I0489176

Walk With Me
Meditations in Nature

Meditations by
Paul Gitto

Photography and book design by
Rebecca V Tower

Acknowledgements

Thank you to all our friends and family, who encouraged us to create another book.

Thank you to everyone who purchased our first book, Keeper of the Flame, still available at amazon.com.

All images and poems are the original work of Rebecca V Tower and Paul Gitto, and may not be copied or used without permission.

Paul's Dedication:
to Stephen and Patty

Rebecca's Dedication:
to Mayfair, Elena, Terrence, and Elise

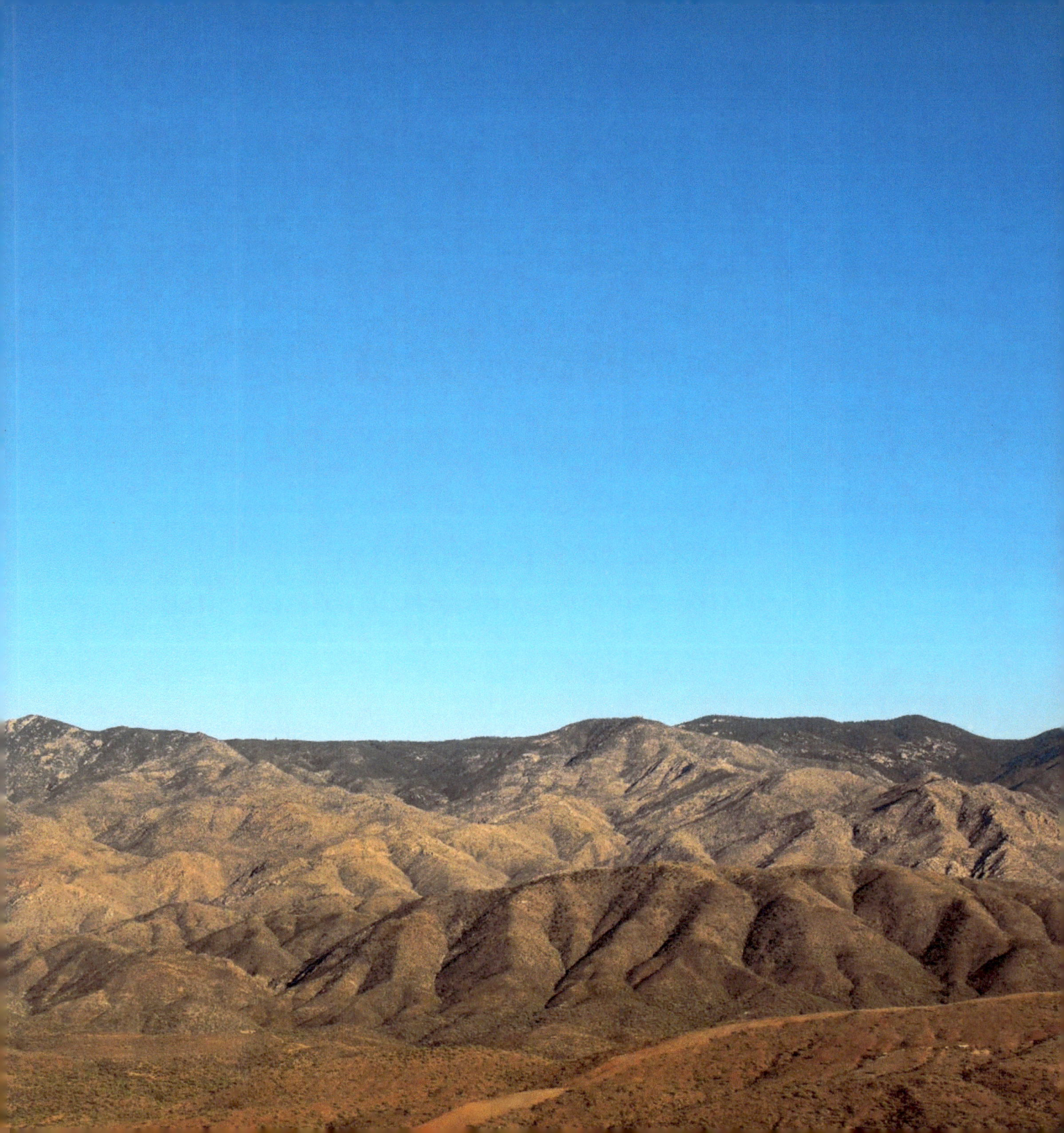

From the
untamed
beauty of
this earth
one can see
God's hand
in all His
creation.

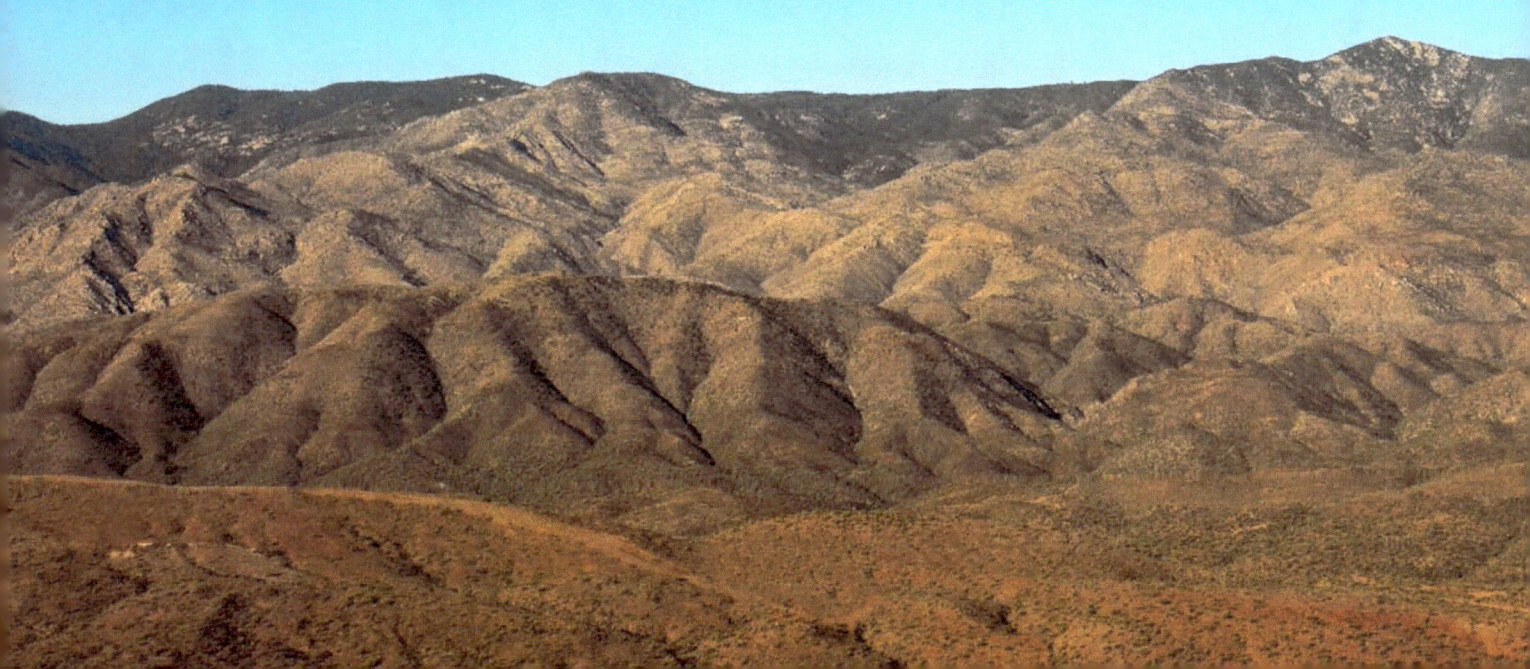

O Lord,
can I be humble
enough
to ask!
It is in the
treasury
of Your heart
that I seek You.
Humbly
I pray,
I will find
You there.

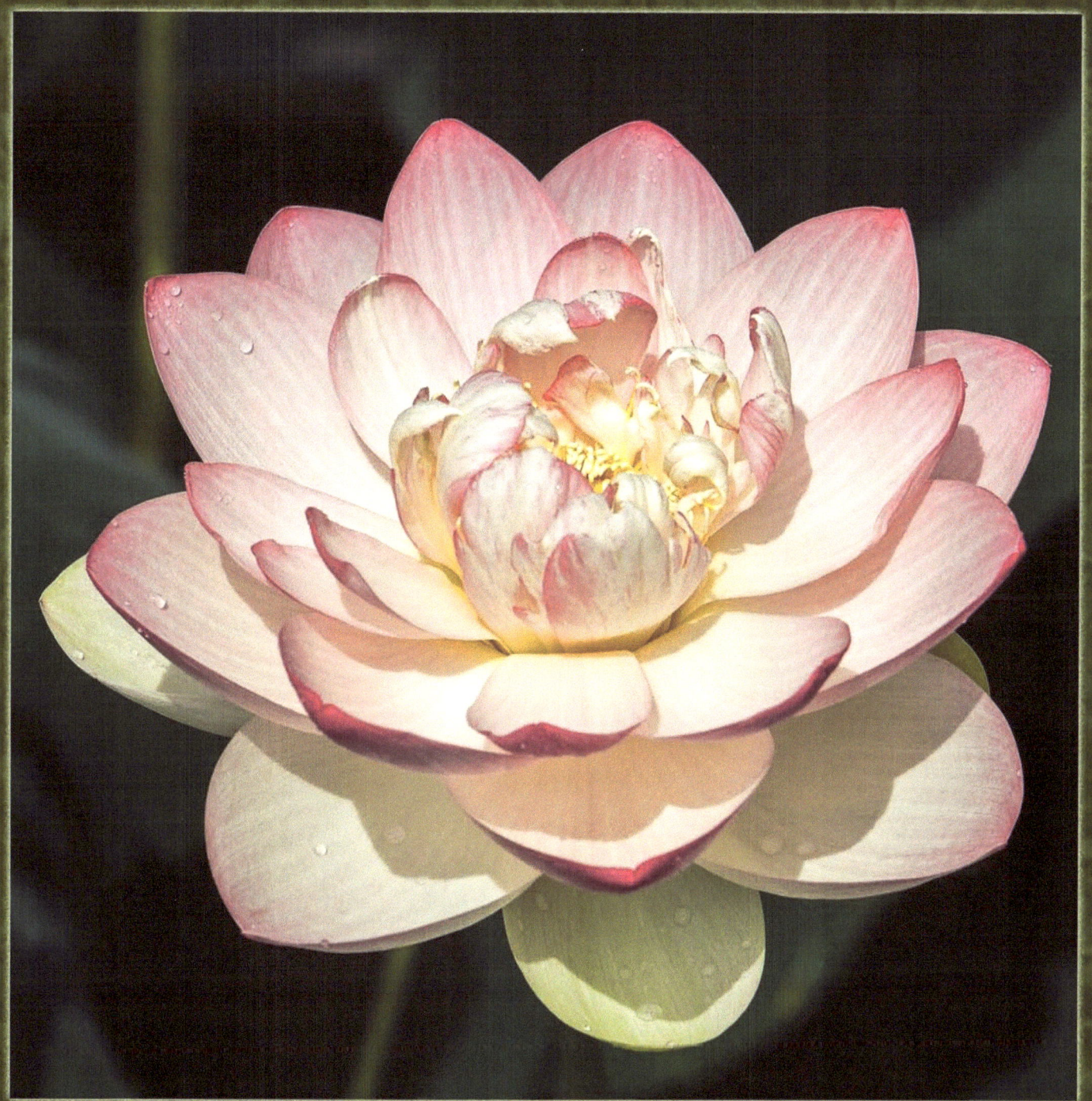

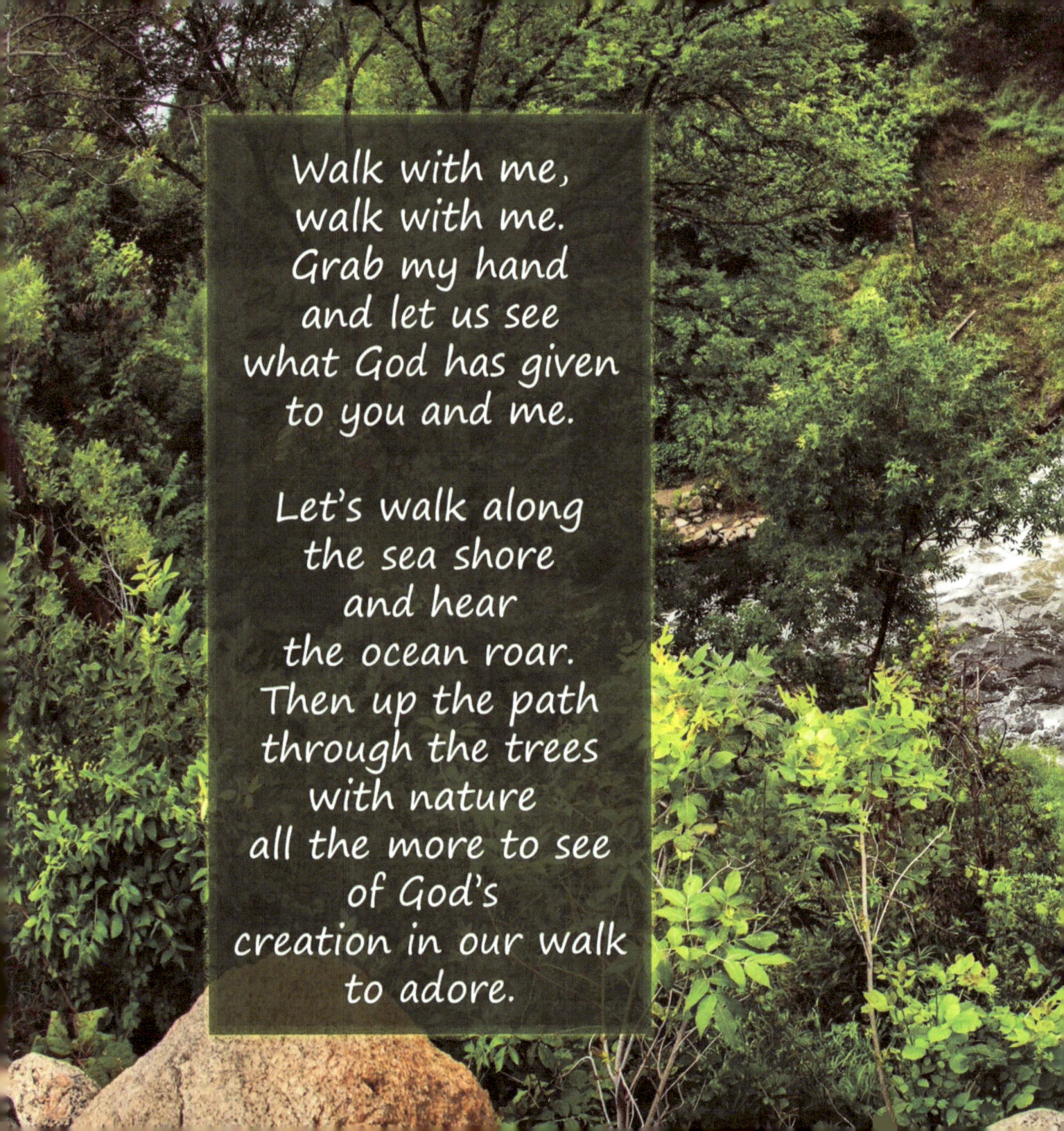

Walk with me,
walk with me.
Grab my hand
and let us see
what God has given
to you and me.

Let's walk along
the sea shore
and hear
the ocean roar.
Then up the path
through the trees
with nature
all the more to see
of God's
creation in our walk
to adore.

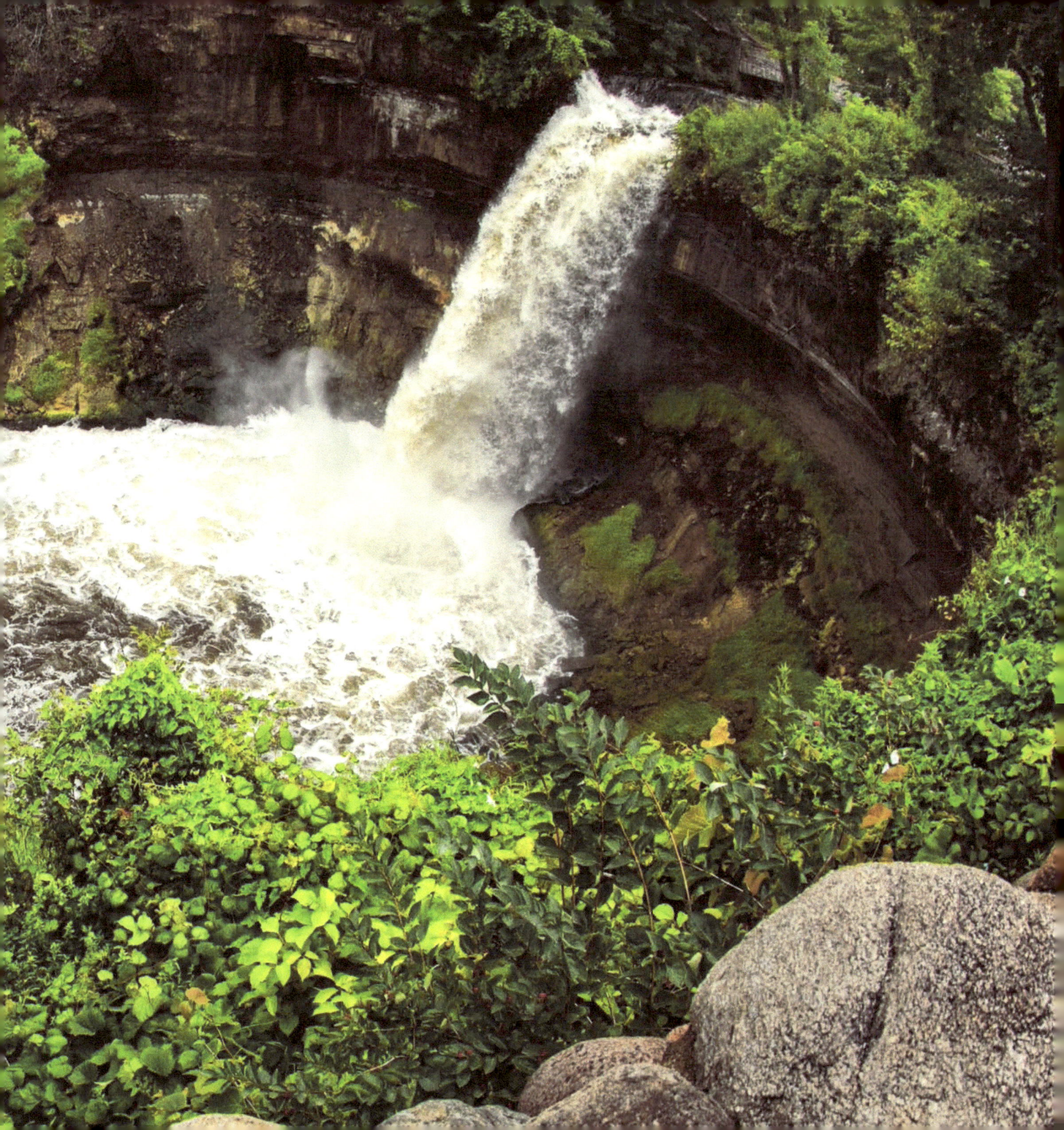

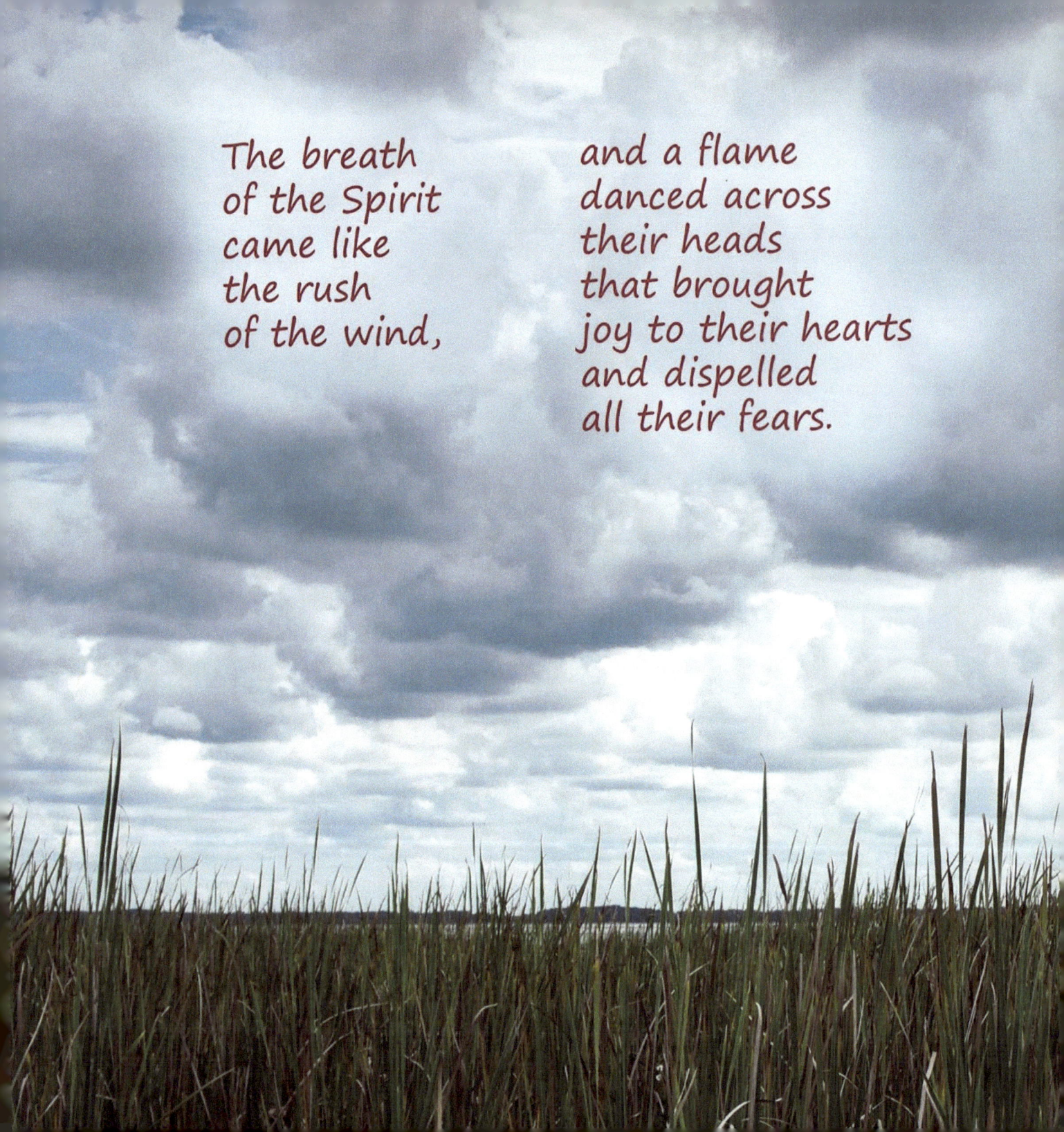

The breath
of the Spirit
came like
the rush
of the wind,

and a flame
danced across
their heads
that brought
joy to their hearts
and dispelled
all their fears.

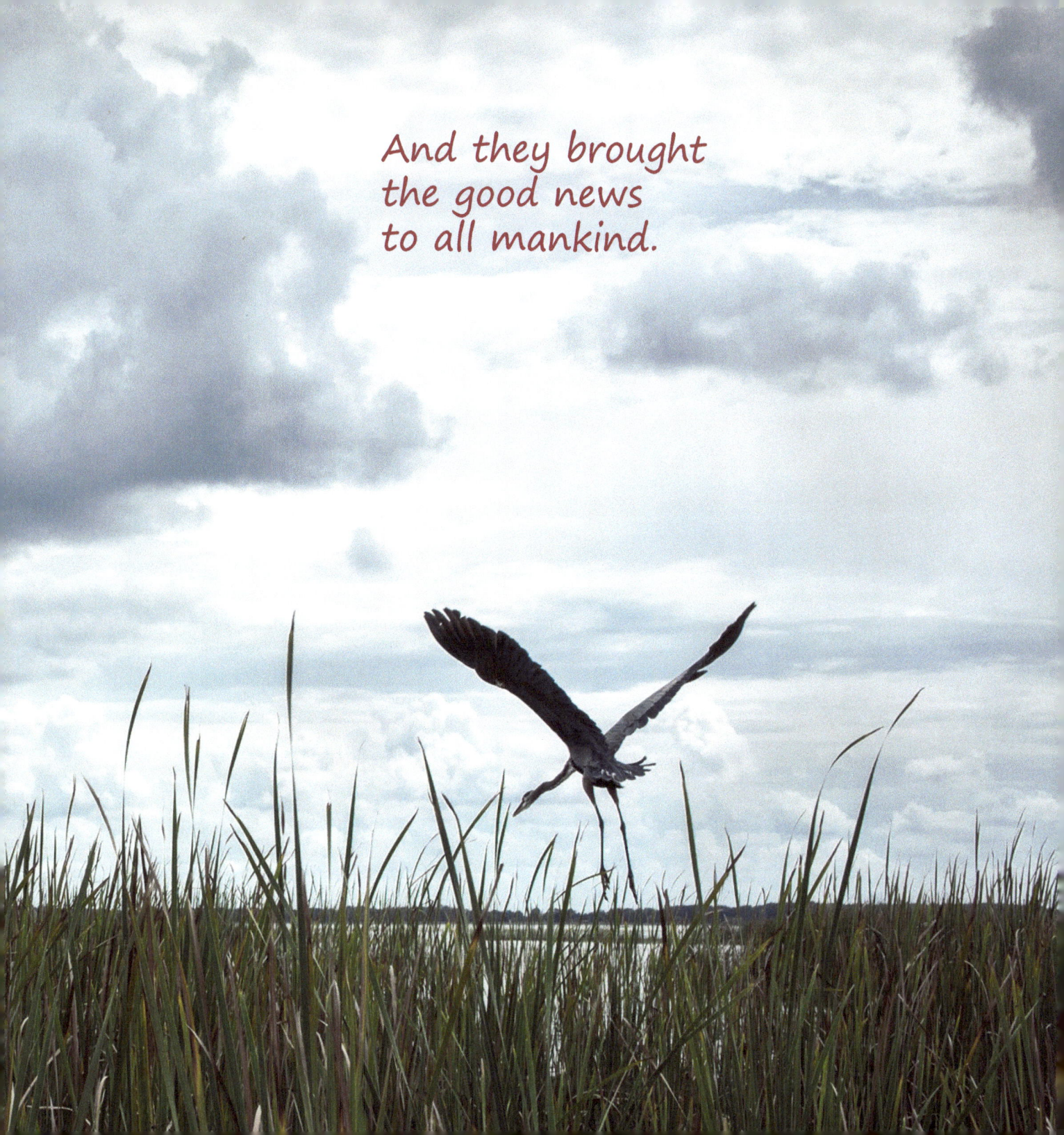

And they brought
the good news
to all mankind.

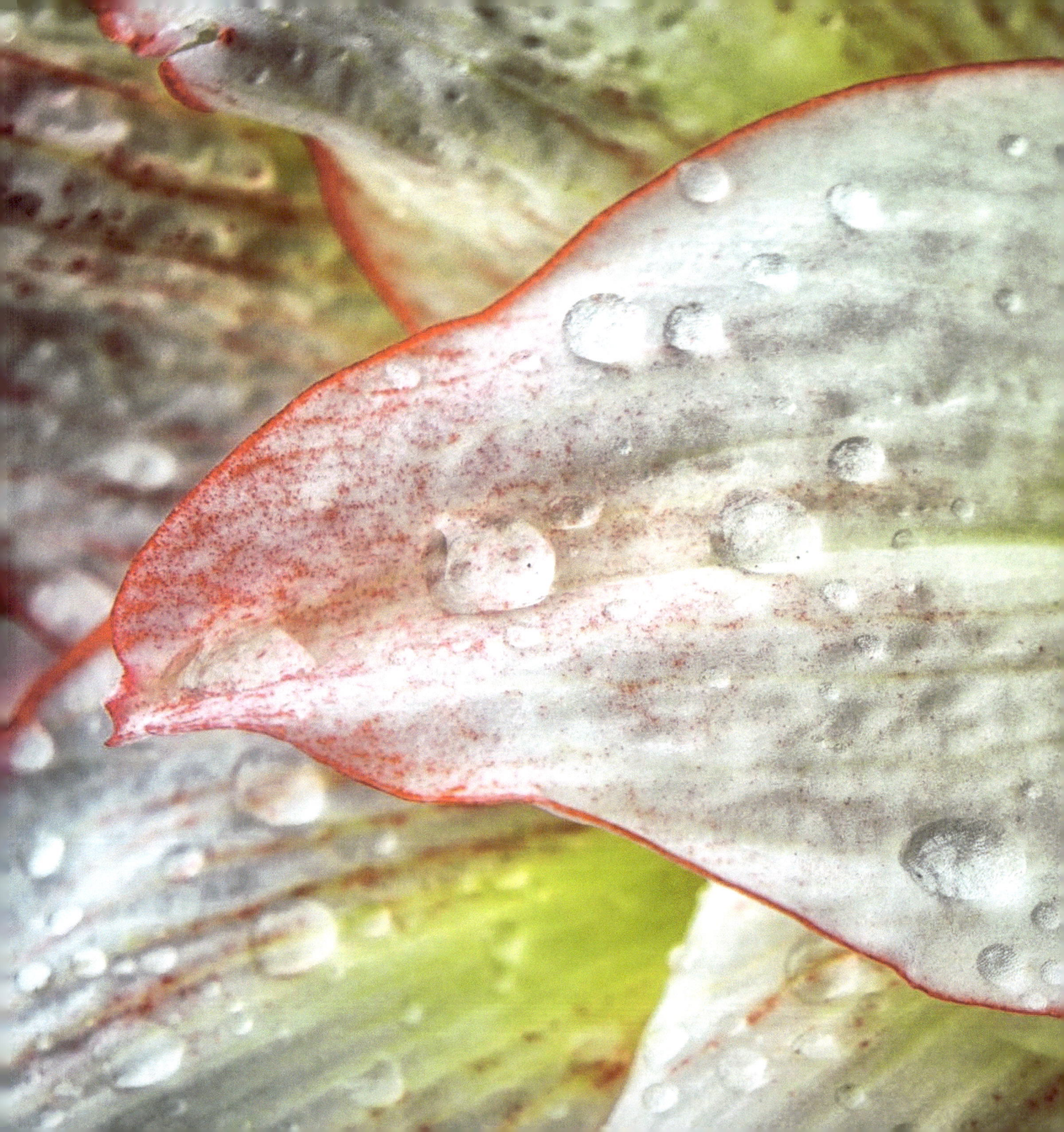

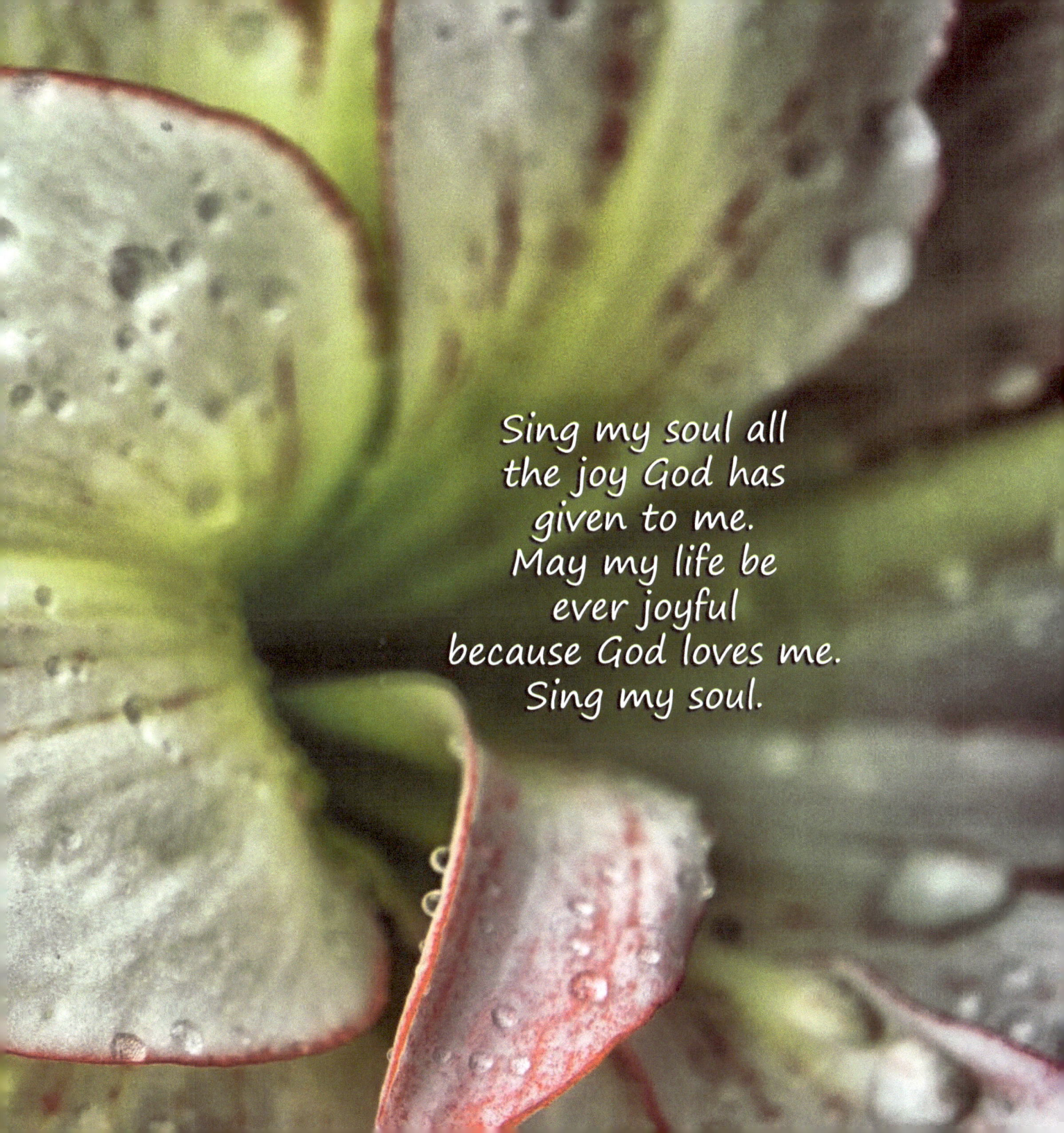

Sing my soul all
the joy God has
given to me.
May my life be
ever joyful
because God loves me.
Sing my soul.

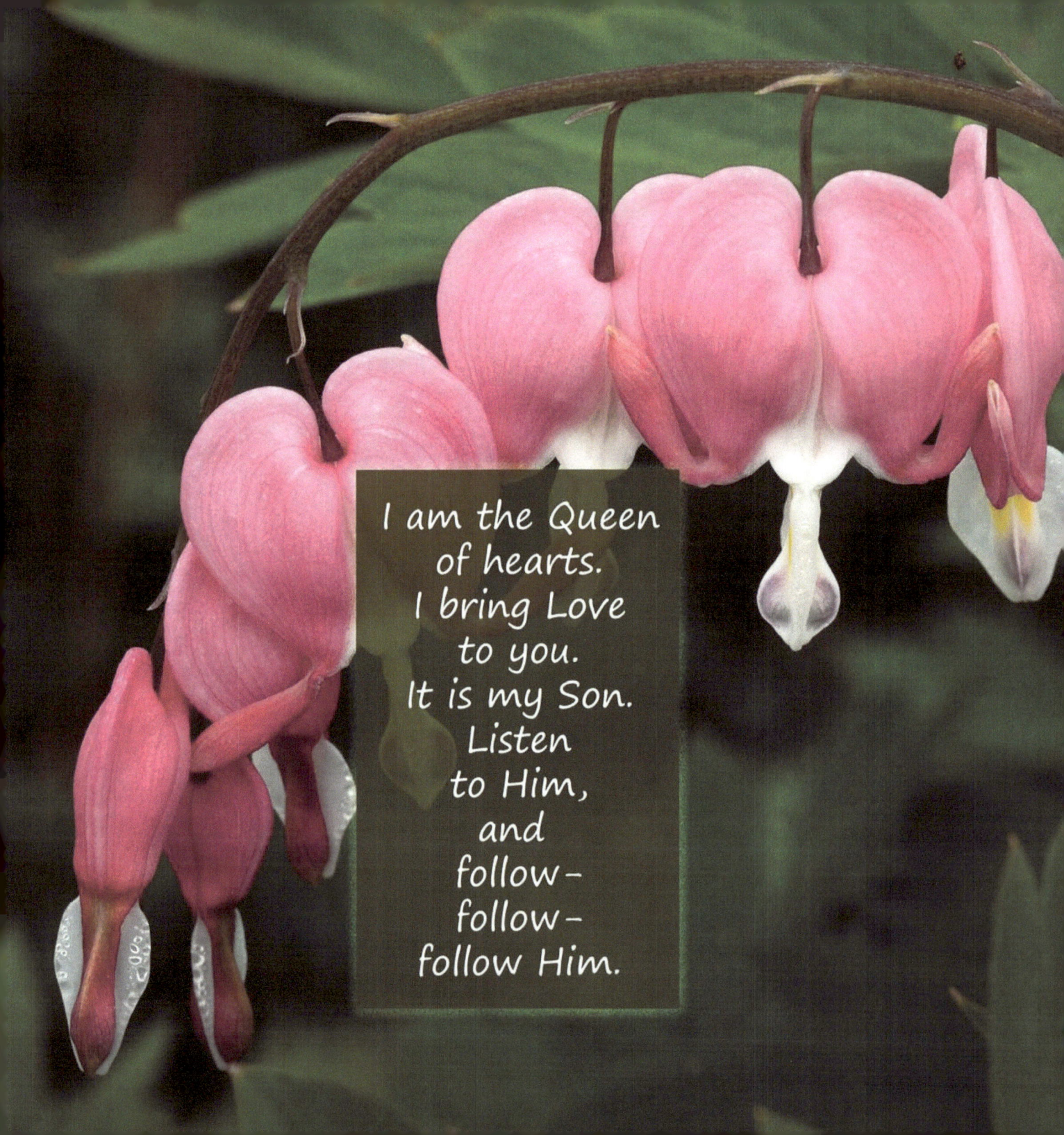

I am the Queen
of hearts.
I bring Love
to you.
It is my Son.
Listen
to Him,
and
follow—
follow—
follow Him.

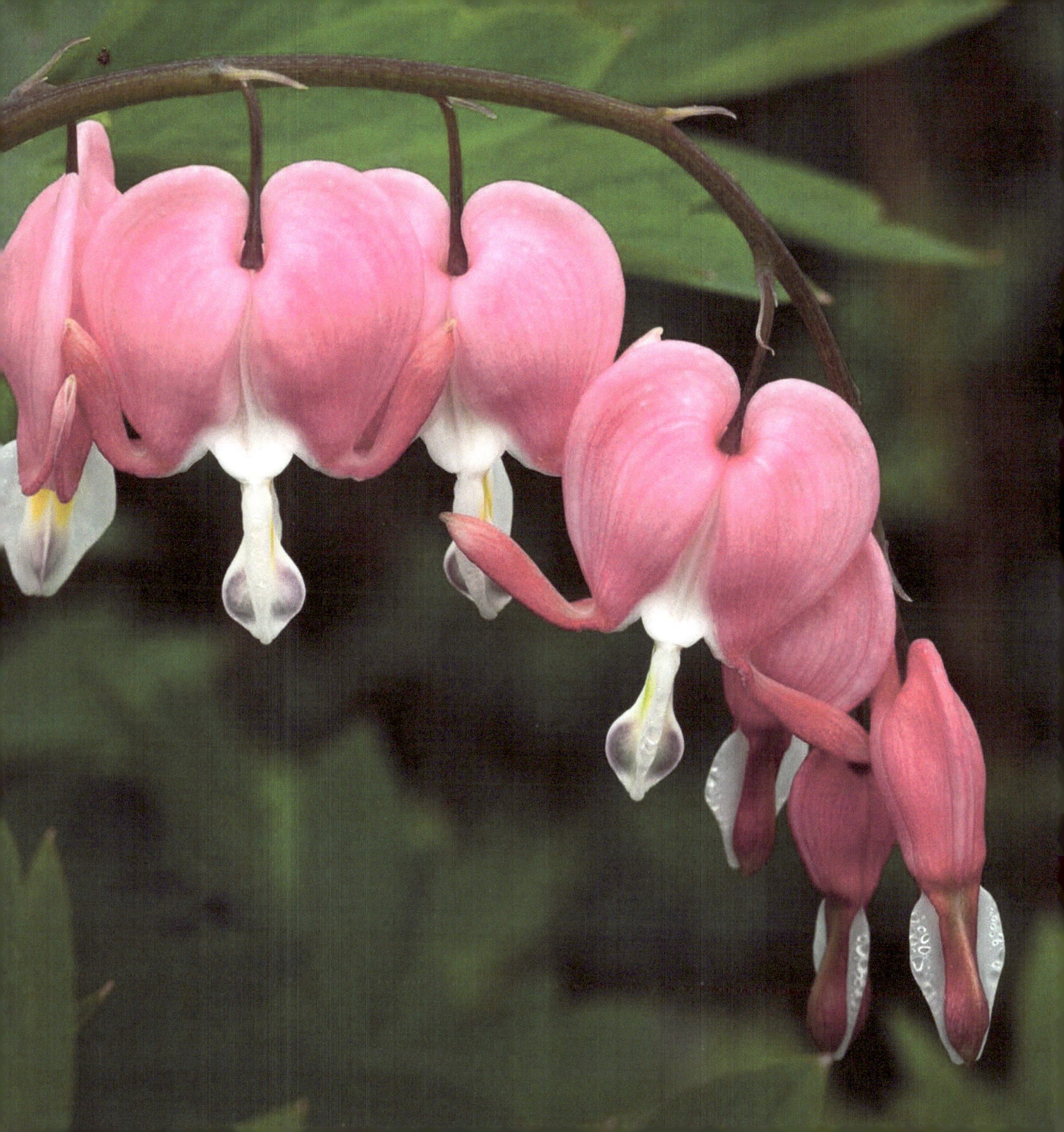

How sweet the Lamb of God,
who has put joy into our
hearts this night.

How sweet the Lamb of God,
whose voice is pearls
bubbling from the sea.

How sweet the Lamb of God,
who came to save the world
and bring love to all mankind.

With angelic sounds of the night,
how sweet is the Lamb of God.
How sweet is He.

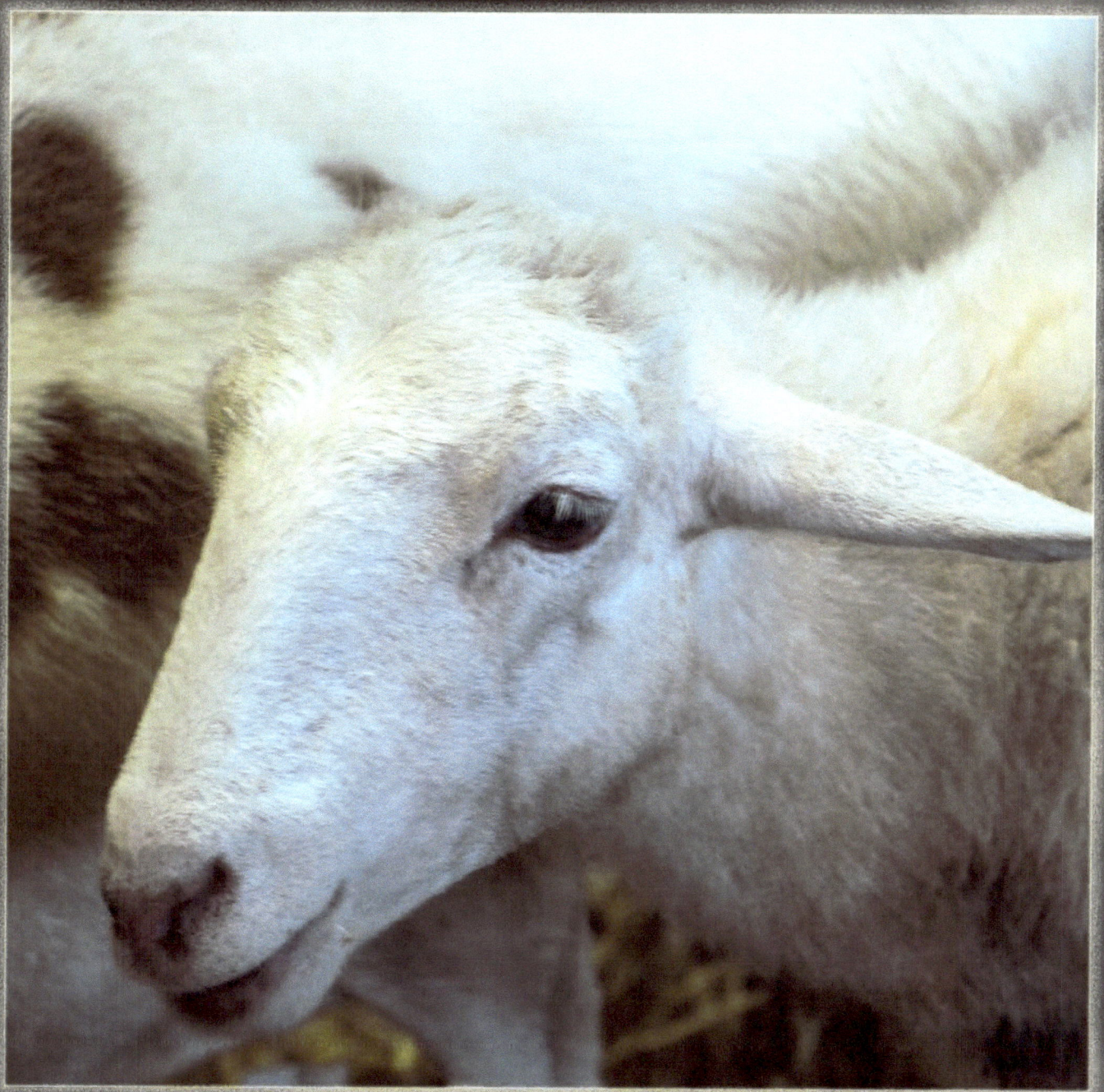

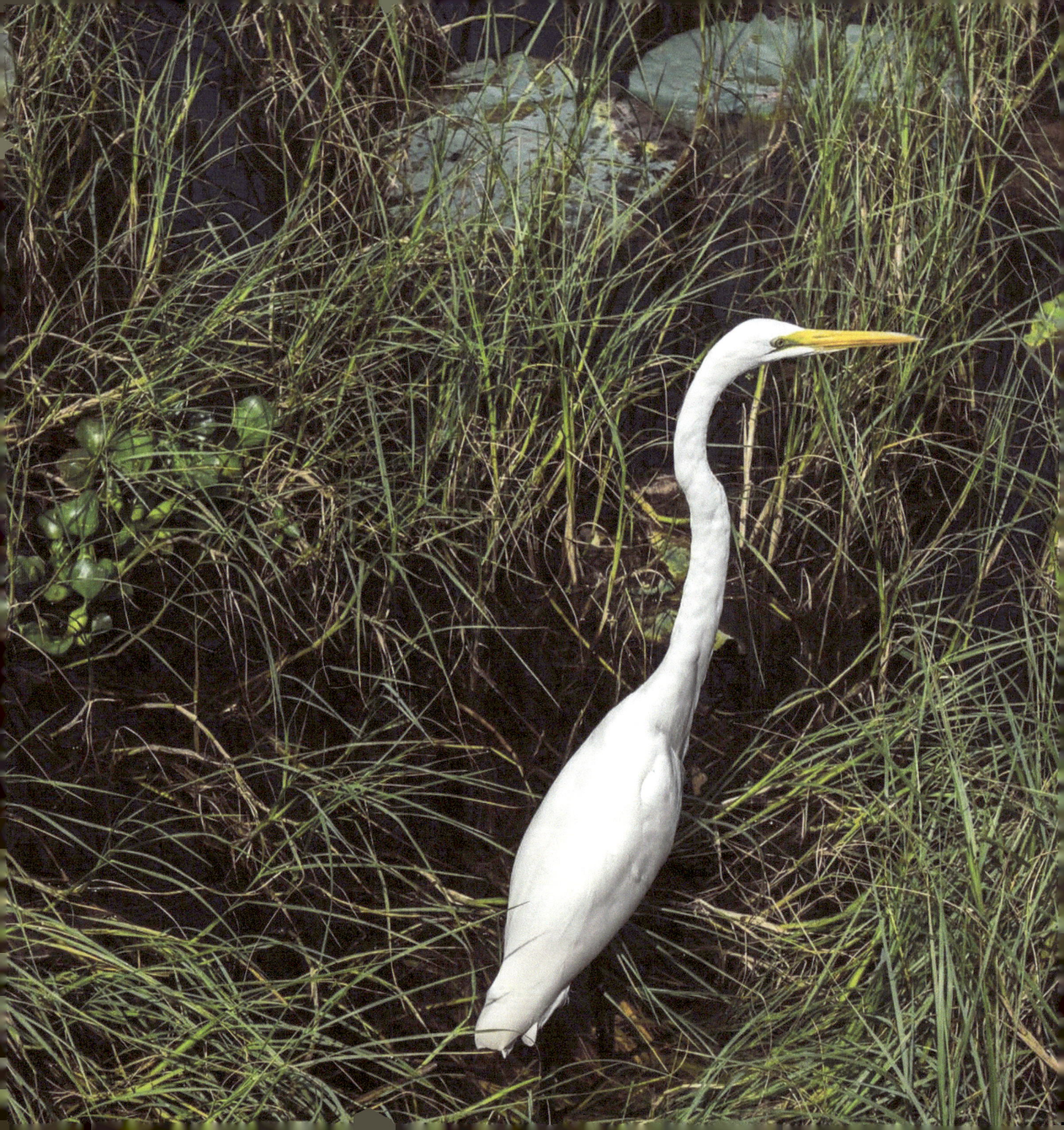

When I go to bed
each night I say
Dear God,
what can I be thankful
for today?

I believe You are
in heaven,
and I did not
profane Your Name.
I pray that I did
Your will today,
as it is done in heaven.

Dear God,
thank you for the food
You gave me today
from your bounty.

Dear God, I pray
I did not sin today.
I know You will
forgive me if I did.
I pray I will forgive,
if someone
offended me.

Dear God,
I am thankful
that I was
not tempted
to do evil today.

Amen

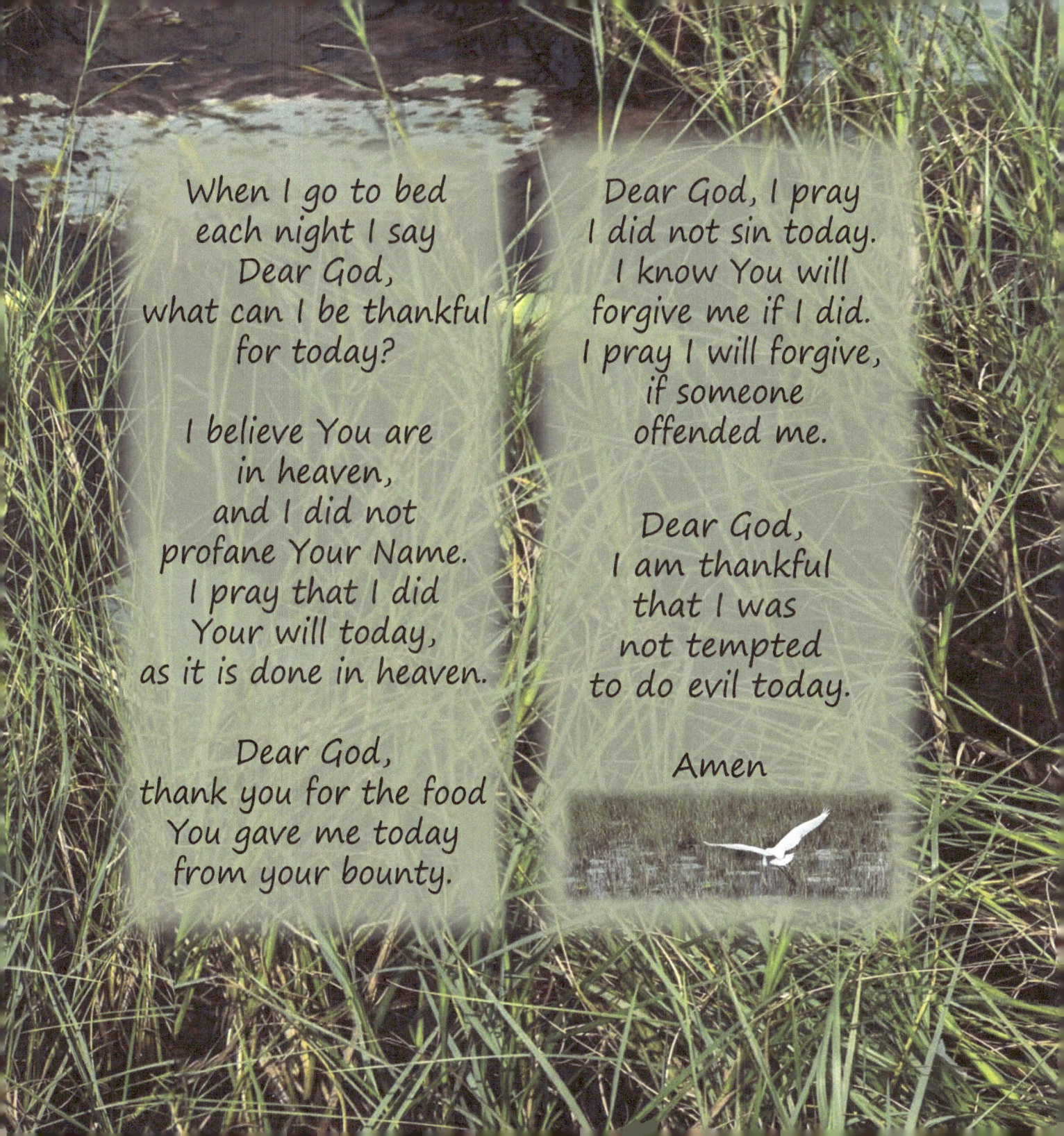

I can hear
the hammer hitting
the nails.
I see the soldiers
lifting the cross.

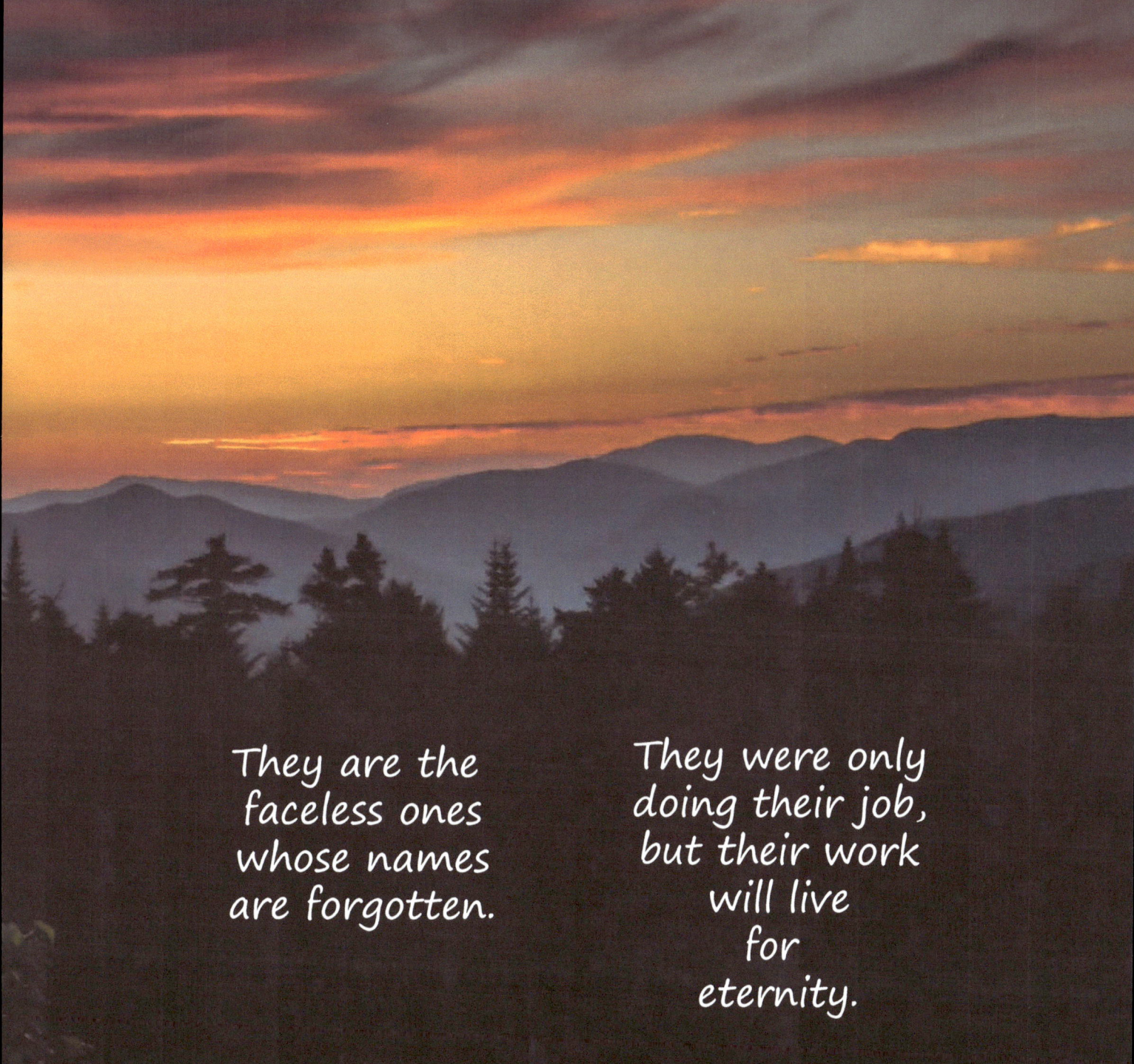

They are the
faceless ones
whose names
are forgotten.

They were only
doing their job,
but their work
will live
for
eternity.

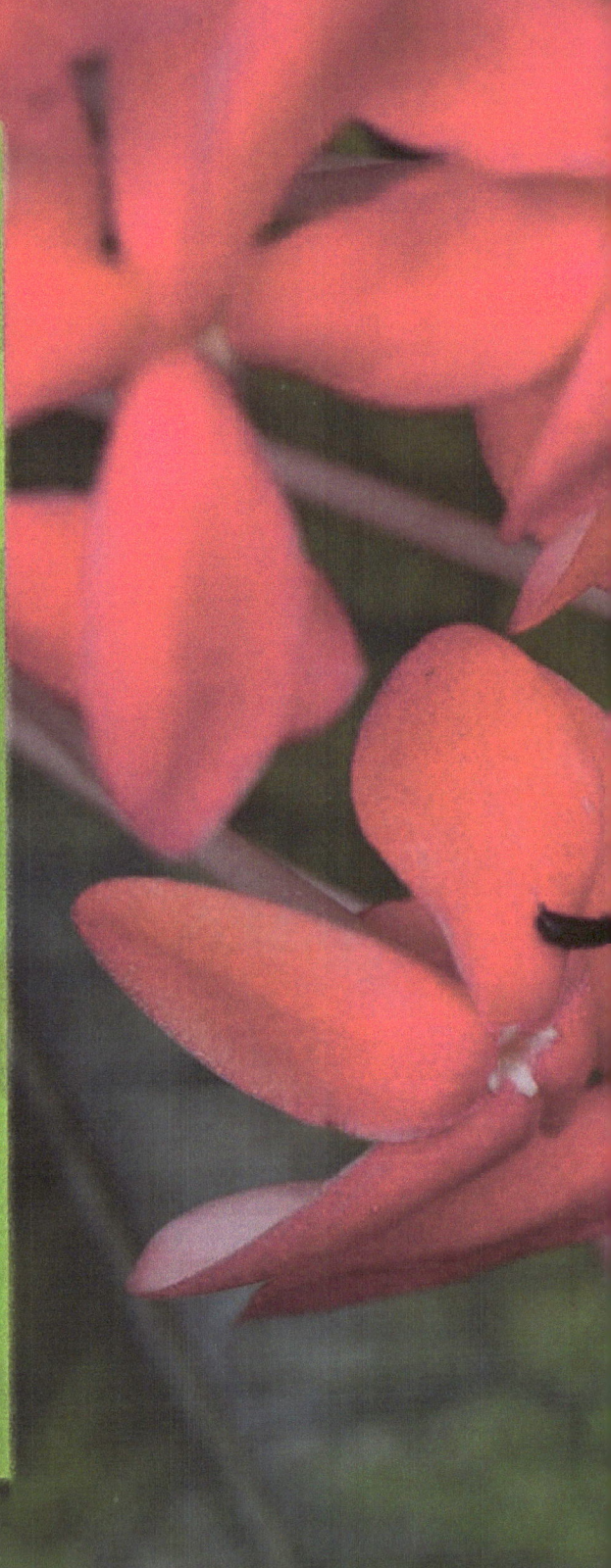

Watching the butterfly
go from flower
to flower
pollinating each one,
I wonder
how God
gives each of us
a unique gift.
Do we ever
give thanks?

I wonder,
should we go out
and pollinate
the good news
to everyone
we meet,
and thank God
for the chance
to do so?

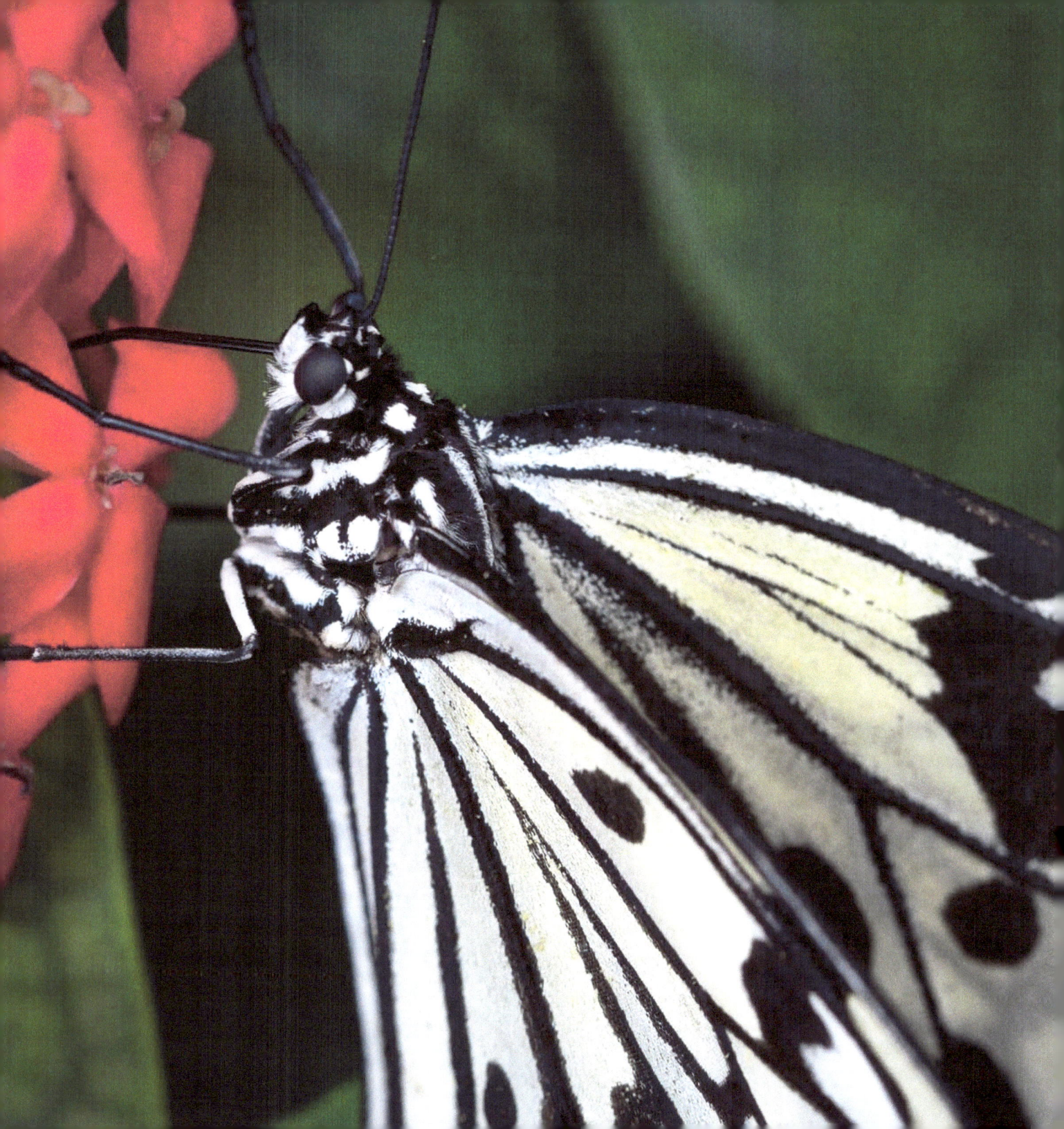

I felt lonely
like rose petals
falling in a fog
early in the morning.

Will the Son
touch my heart today
and lift the fog,
and bring love
into my life?

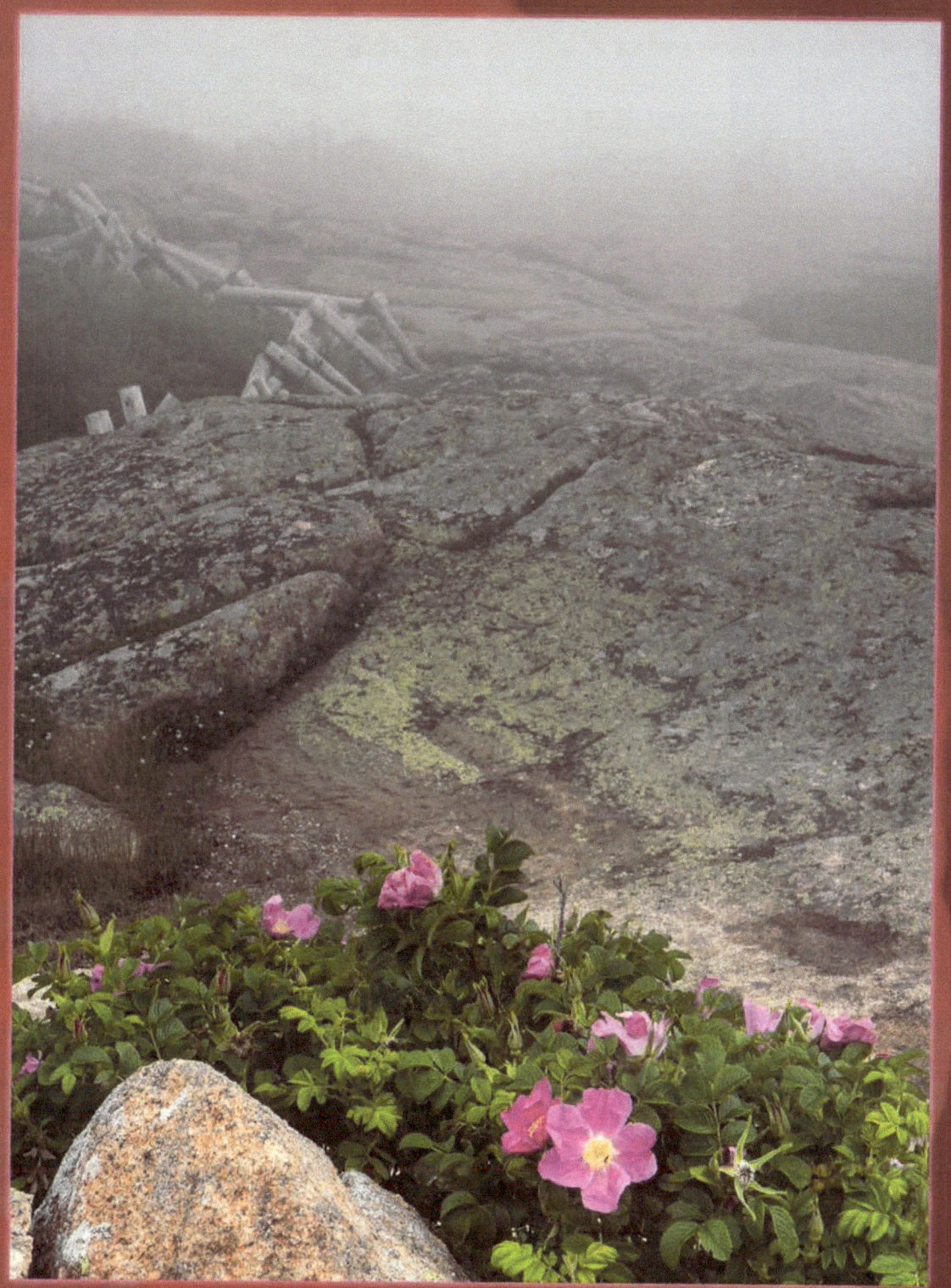

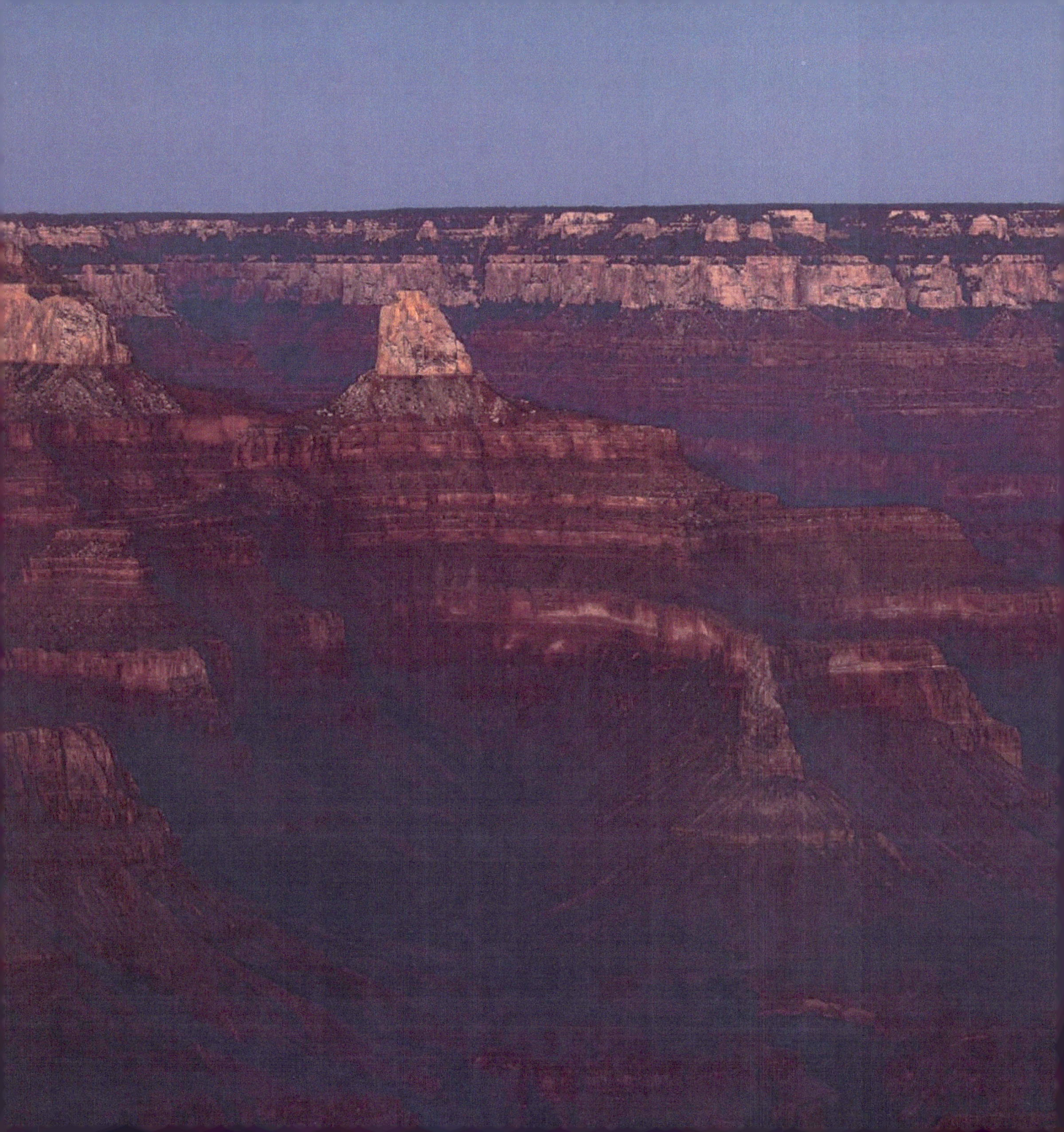

Lord, if it is
truly You,
give me
the courage
to come to You.
Give me Your hand
and lead me
through the dark
night
into the light.

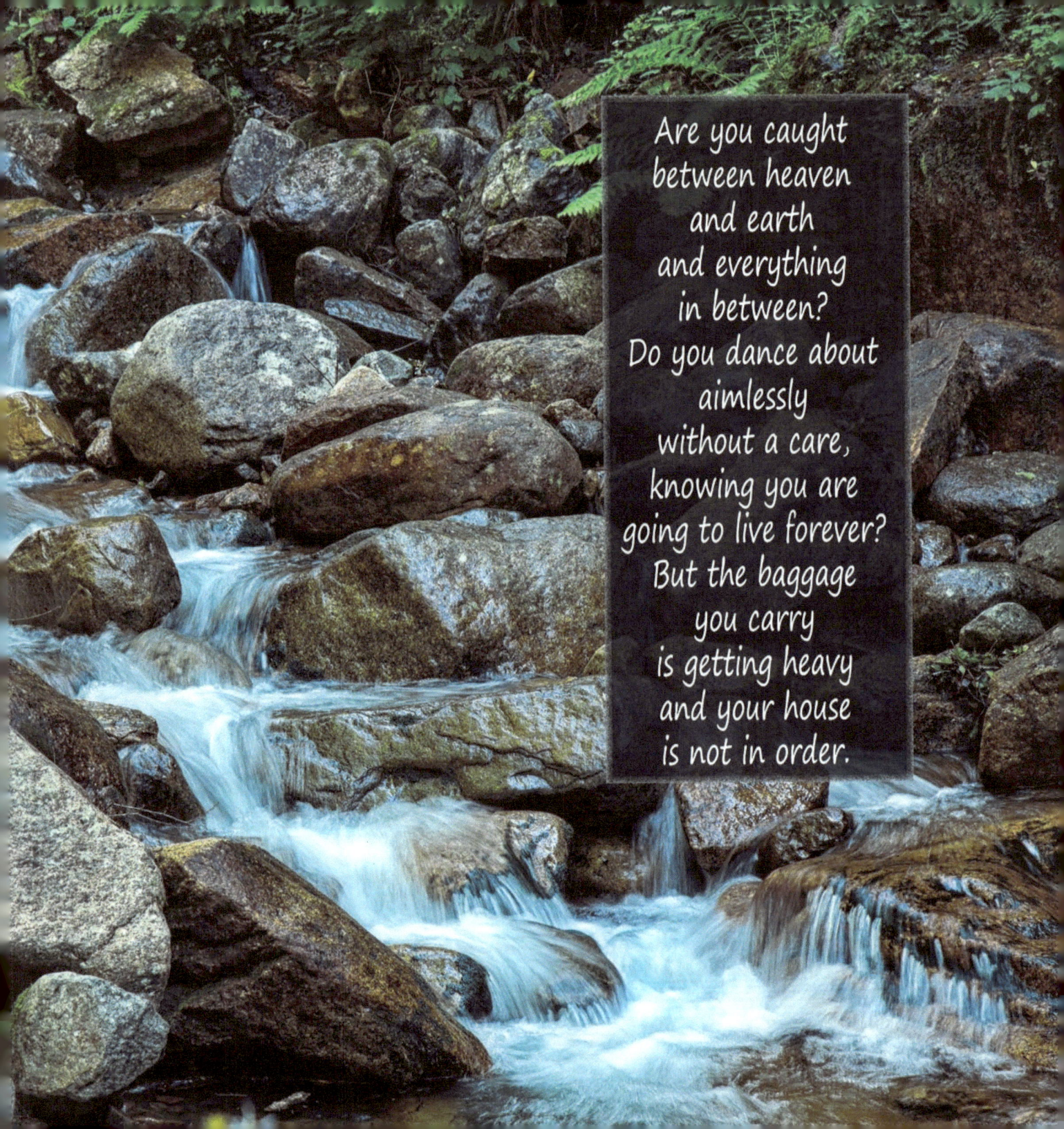

Are you caught
between heaven
and earth
and everything
in between?
Do you dance about
aimlessly
without a care,
knowing you are
going to live forever?
But the baggage
you carry
is getting heavy
and your house
is not in order.

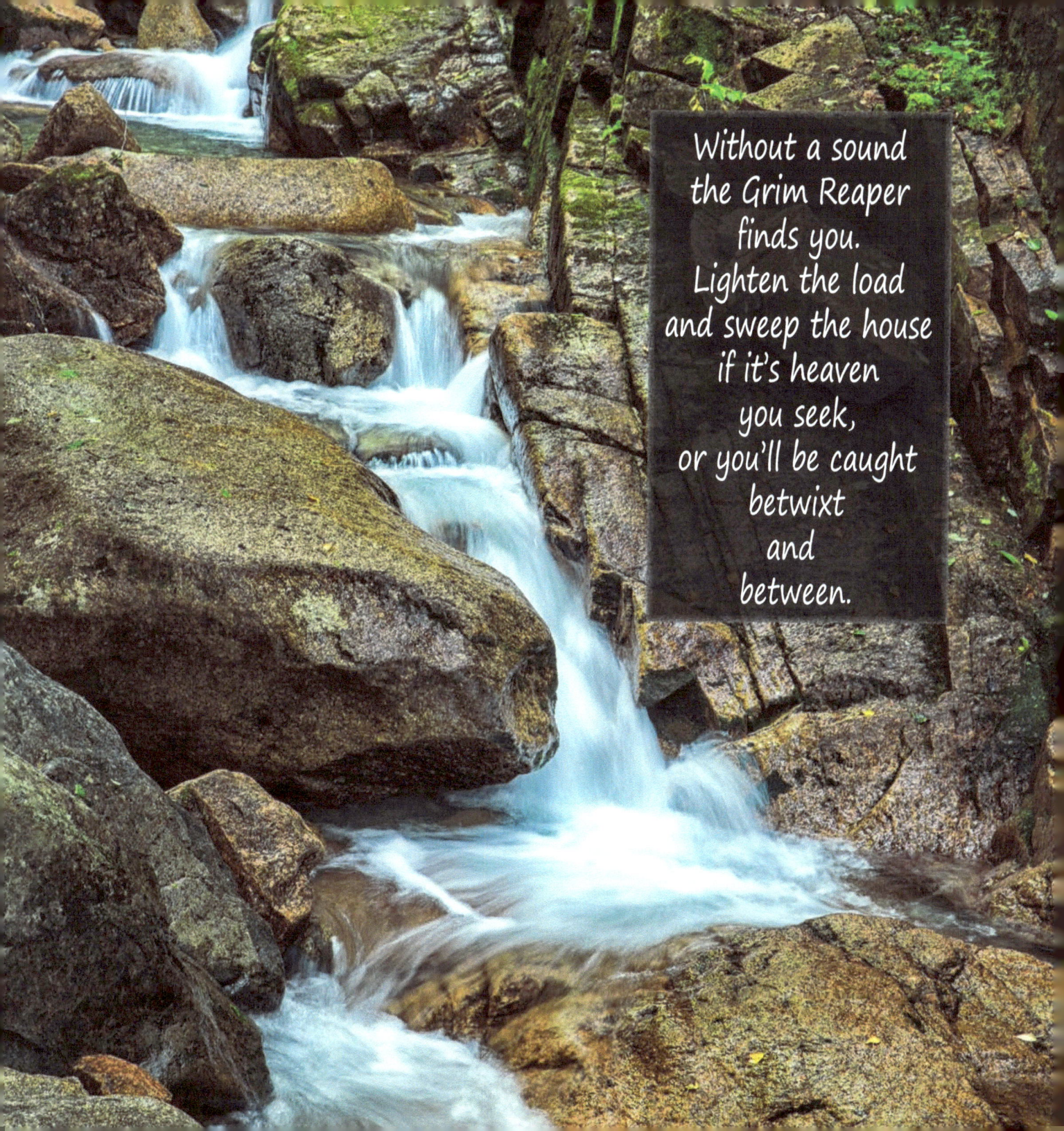

Without a sound
the Grim Reaper
finds you.
Lighten the load
and sweep the house
if it's heaven
you seek,
or you'll be caught
betwixt
and
between.

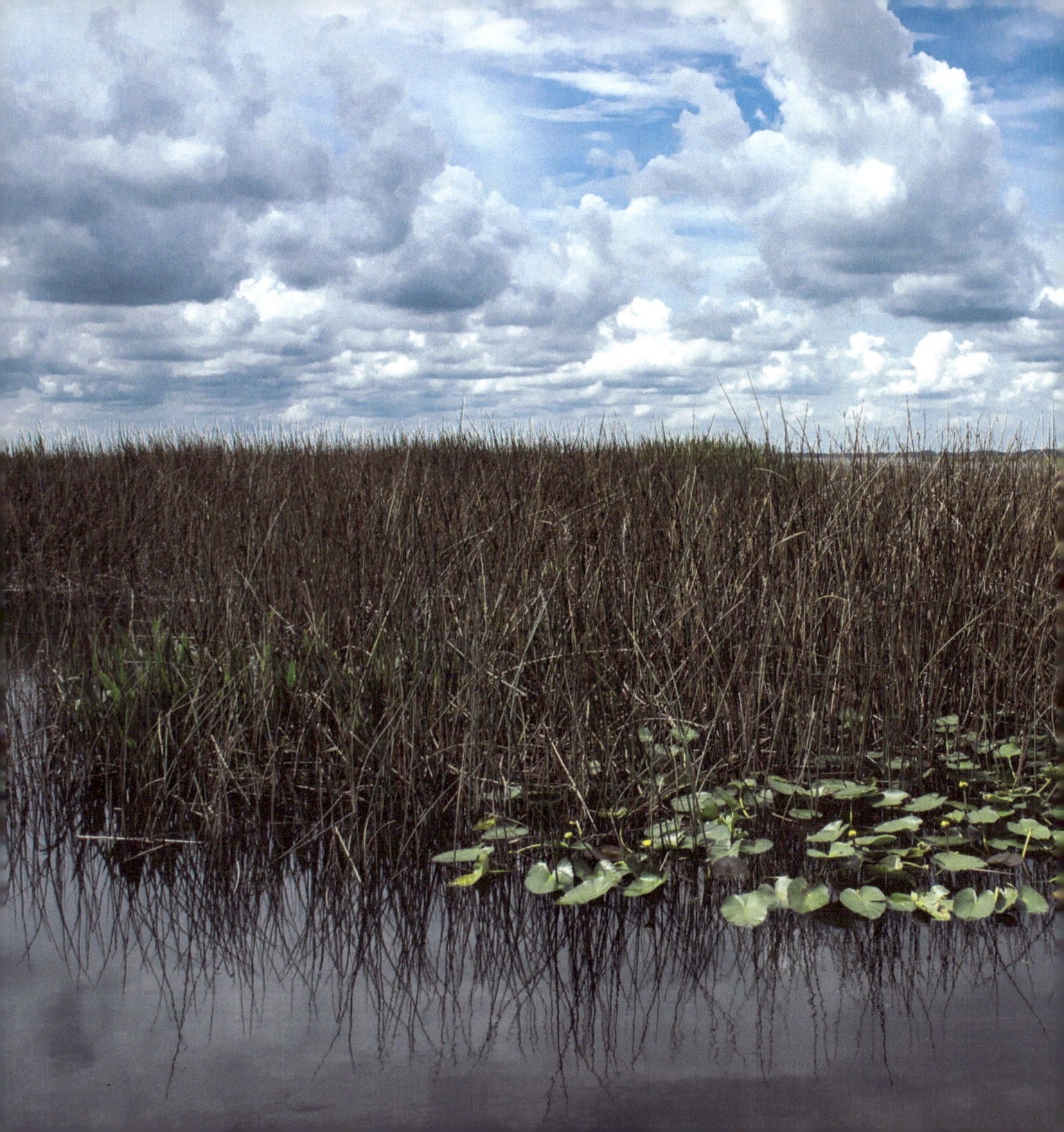

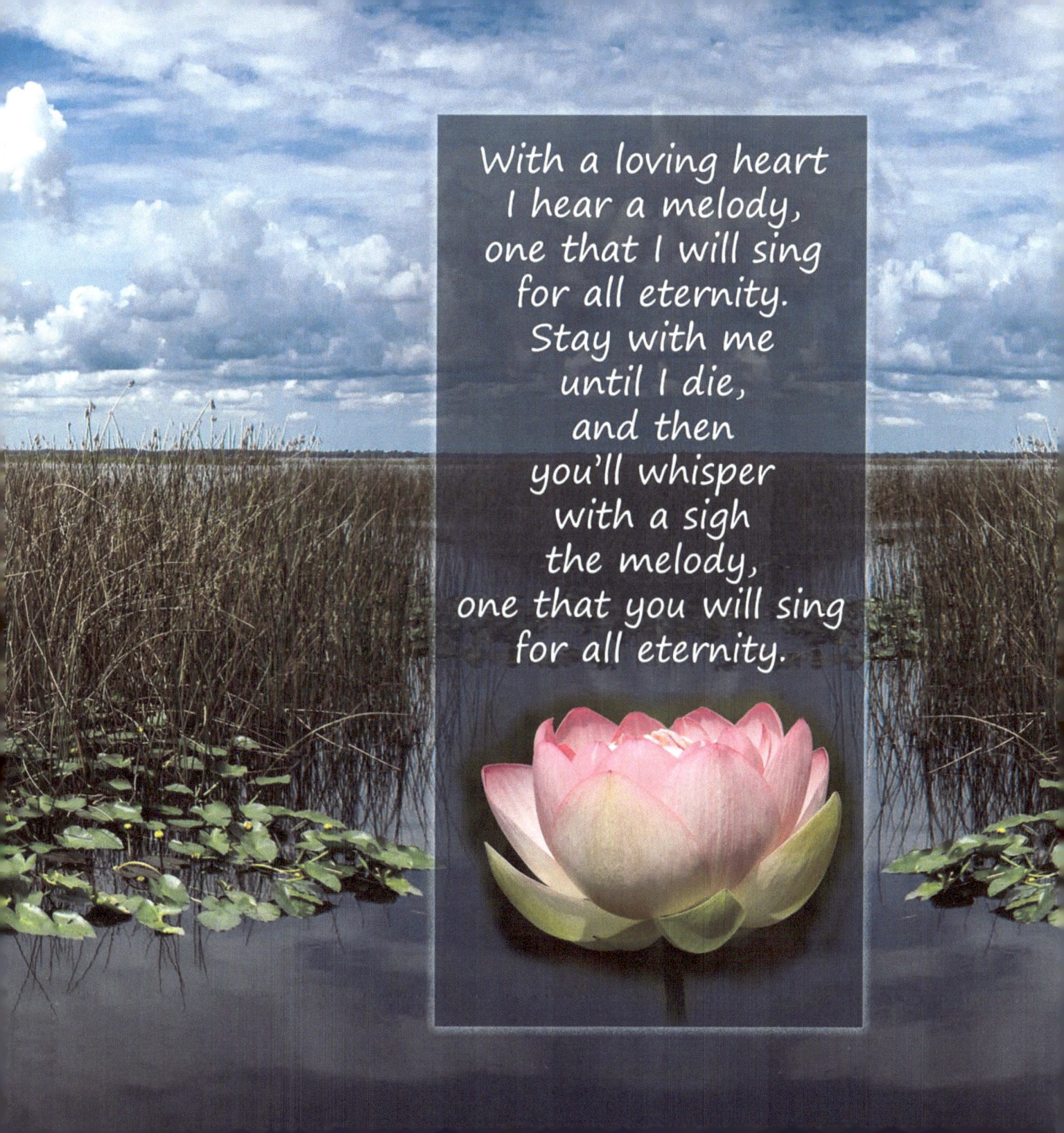

With a loving heart
I hear a melody,
one that I will sing
for all eternity.
Stay with me
until I die,
and then
you'll whisper
with a sigh
the melody,
one that you will sing
for all eternity.

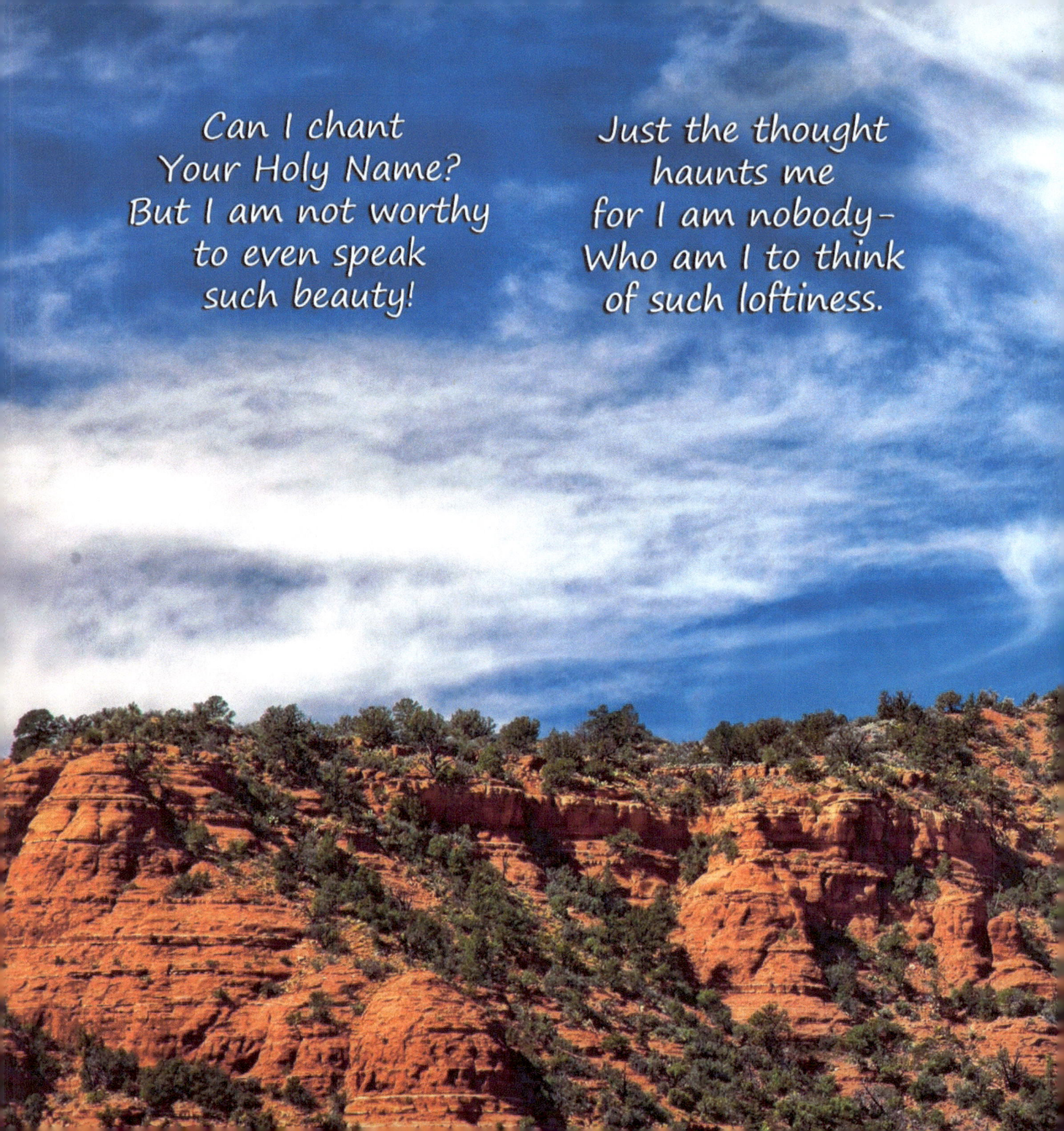

Can I chant
Your Holy Name?
But I am not worthy
to even speak
such beauty!

Just the thought
haunts me
for I am nobody –
Who am I to think
of such loftiness.

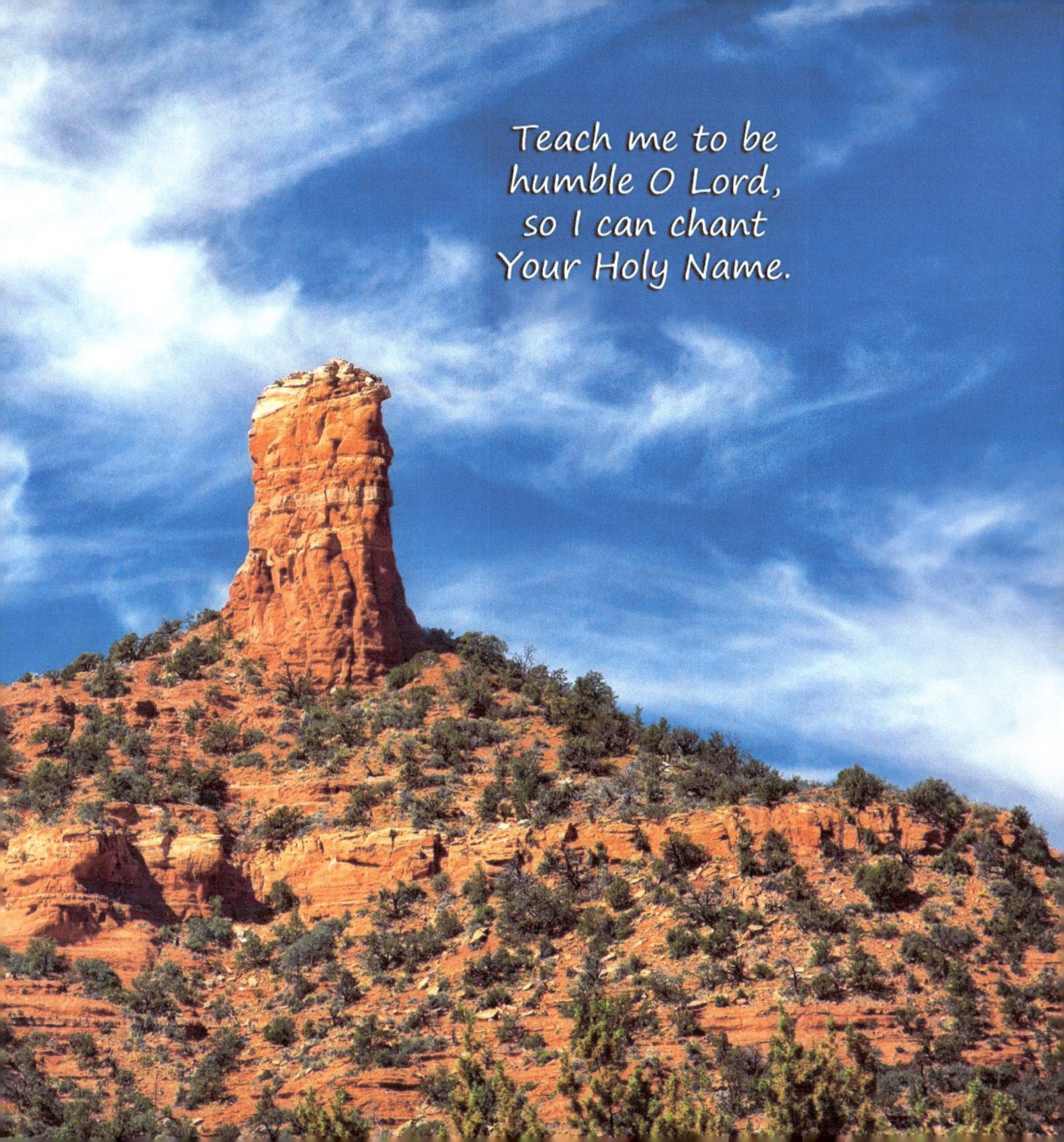

Teach me to be
humble O Lord,
so I can chant
Your Holy Name.

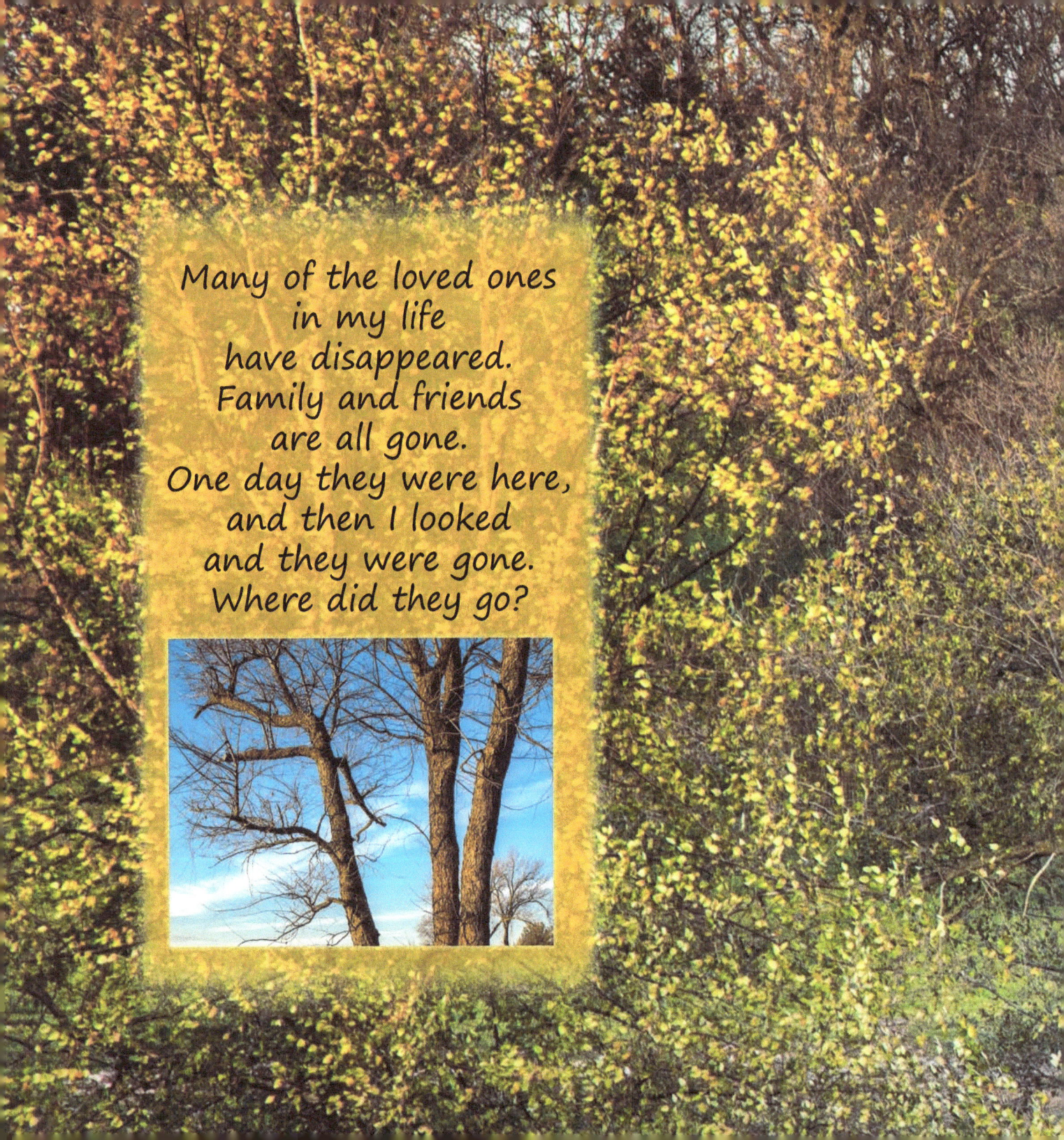

Many of the loved ones
in my life
have disappeared.
Family and friends
are all gone.
One day they were here,
and then I looked
and they were gone.
Where did they go?

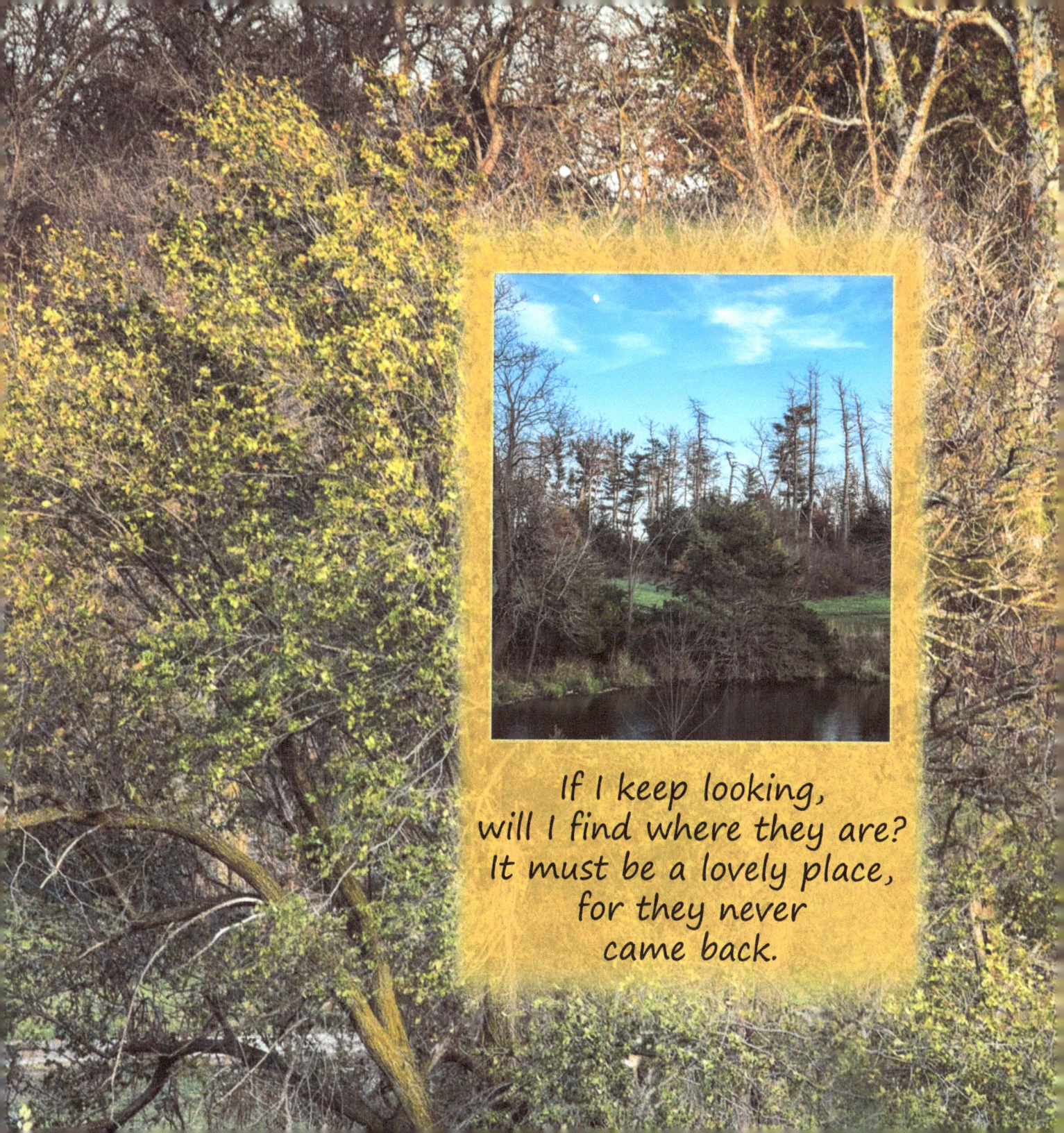

If I keep looking,
will I find where they are?
It must be a lovely place,
for they never
came back.

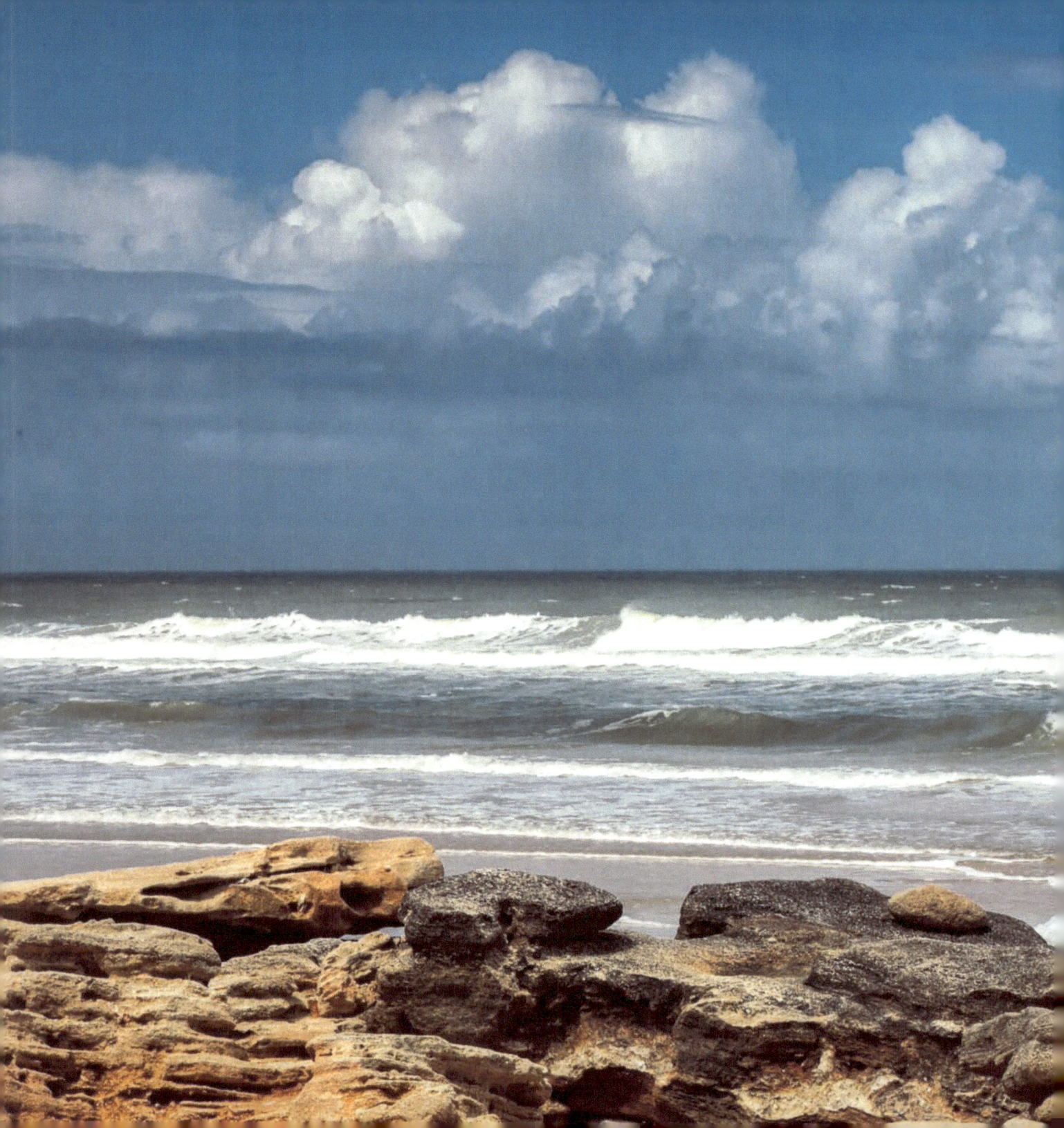

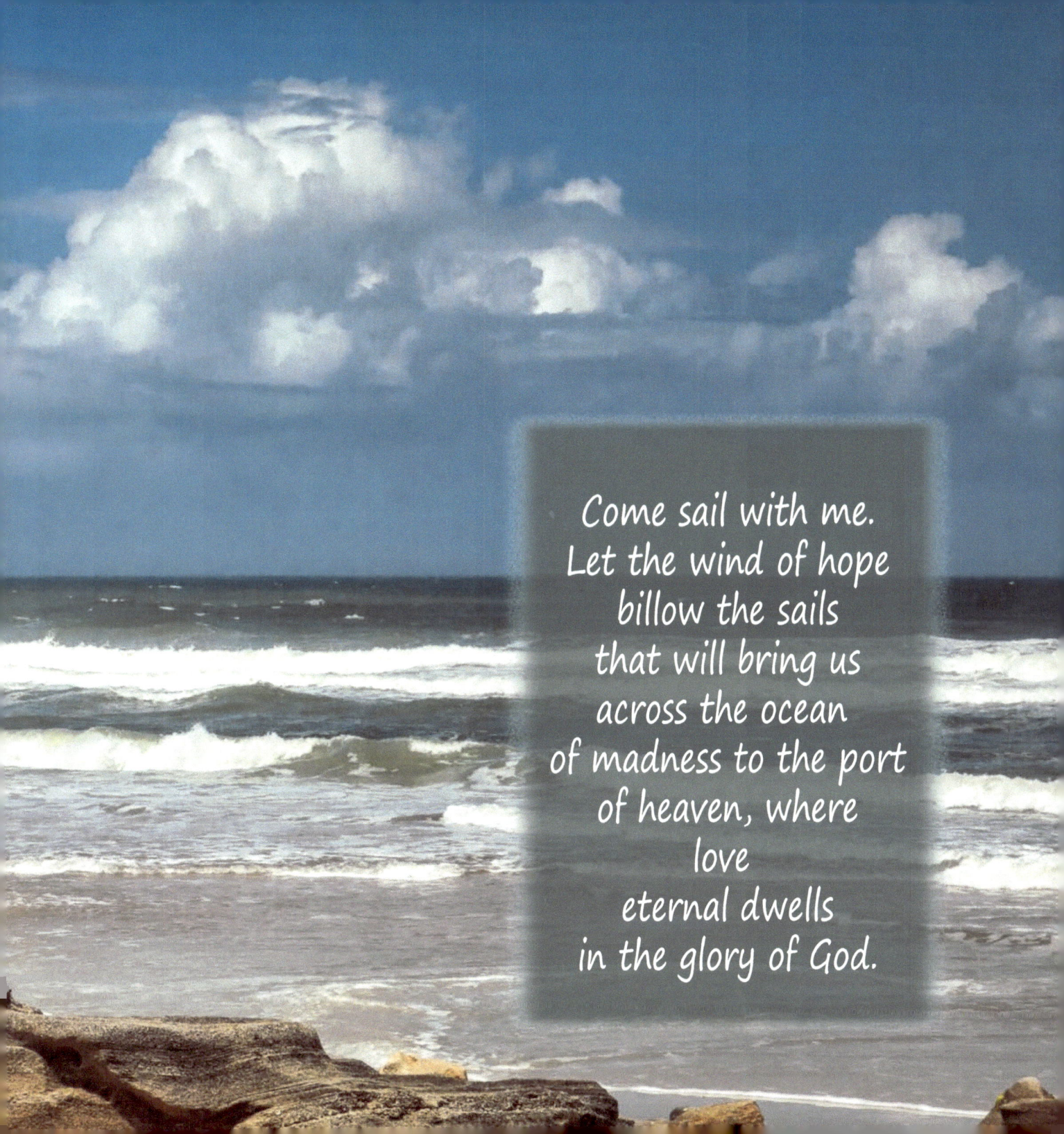

Come sail with me.
Let the wind of hope
billow the sails
that will bring us
across the ocean
of madness to the port
of heaven, where
love
eternal dwells
in the glory of God.

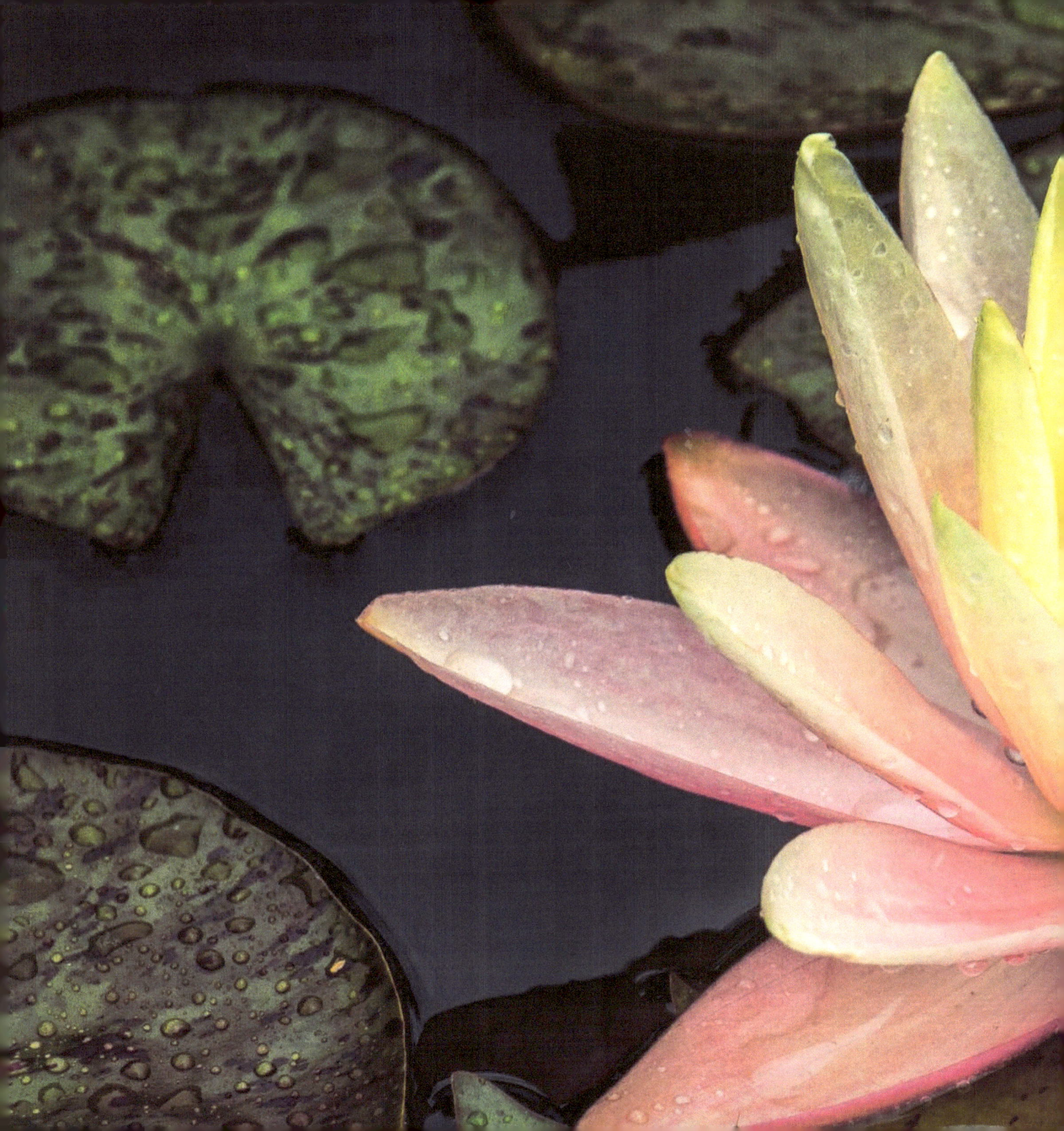

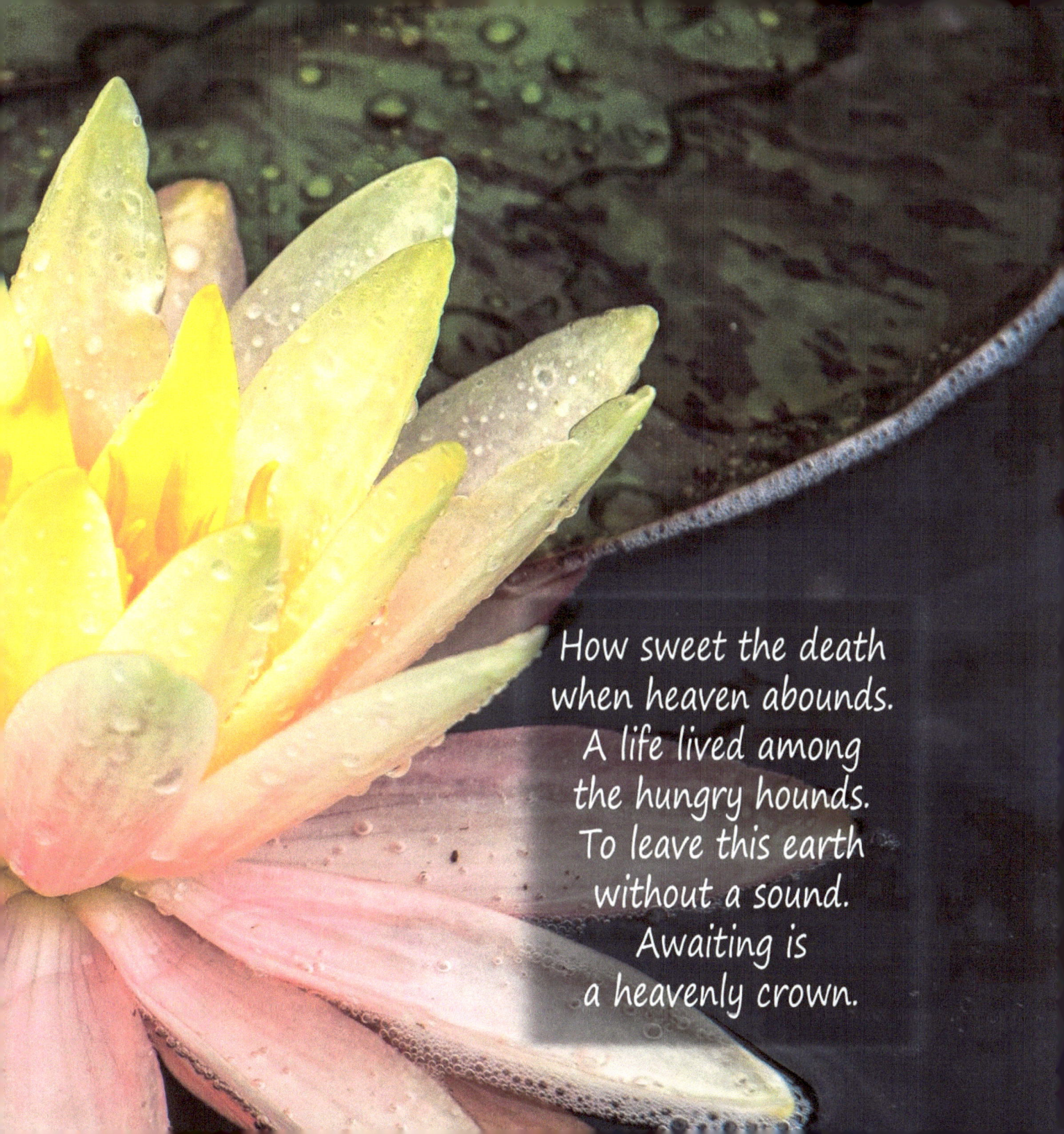

How sweet the death
when heaven abounds.
A life lived among
the hungry hounds.
To leave this earth
without a sound.
Awaiting is
a heavenly crown.

About the Authors

Paul Gitto is an author of children's books. He also enjoys creating a variety of ceramic items, which he fires in his own kiln.

Rebecca V Tower is a free-lance photographer and graphic designer. She enjoys working on a wide variety of assignments.

We hope this book inspires and gives hope to our readers, and leads them to see the beauty that is all around them. Above all, we hope it gives them ideas to ponder, and brings them closer to God.

www.ingramcontent.com/pod-product-compliance
Lightning Source LLC
Chambersburg PA
CBHW050841180526
45159CB00004B/1981